Otherness and Ethics

Otherness and Ethics

An Ethical Discourse of Levinas and Confucius (Kongzi)

ShinHyung Seong

WIPF & STOCK · Eugene, Oregon

OTHERNESS AND ETHICS
An Ethical Discourse of Levinas and Confucius (Kongzi)

Copyright © 2018 ShinHyung Seong. All rights reserved. Except for brief quotations in critical publications or reviews, no part of this book may be reproduced in any manner without prior written permission from the publisher. Write: Permissions, Wipf and Stock Publishers, 199 W. 8th Ave., Suite 3, Eugene, OR 97401.

Wipf & Stock
An Imprint of Wipf and Stock Publishers
199 W. 8th Ave., Suite 3
Eugene, OR 97401

www.wipfandstock.com

PAPERBACK ISBN: 978-1-5326-4763-5
HARDCOVER ISBN: 978-1-5326-4764-2
EBOOK ISBN: 978-1-5326-4765-9

Manufactured in the U.S.A.

I dedicate this book to my wife, Sooyoung Kim.

Contents

Acknowledgments | ix
Introduction | xi

Part I. Theoretical Foundation on Ethics and Otherness | 1
  1. Reciprocity and the Radical Otherness | 3

Part II. Emmanuel Levinas | 19
  2. The Face of the Other | 23
  3. The Same and the Other | 39
  4. Ethics, Responsibility, and the Human Reality | 53

Part III. Confucius (Kongzi) and the *Analects* | 67
  5. *Ren* and Humanness | 73
  6. Humanness (*Ren*) and Others | 88
  7. *Ren* and Ethics | 102

Part IV. The Ethics of Otherness in Levinas and Kongzi | 117
  8. Kongzi vs. Levinas | 119
  9. The Ethics of Otherness: *Response-ability* and the Narrative of Virtue | 130

Conclusion | 138

Bibliography | 143

Acknowledgments

THIS IS THE MOST joyful moment for me to say "thank you" to those who have supported my writing and to express how grateful I am for all those who have supported my work, not only academically, but also spiritually and mentally. To begin with, I have to express my appreciation to those who aided my academic improvement. Dr. Brent Waters, advised my scholarship, inspired me to ask the significance of otherness in the study of ethics. He encouraged me to ask the question of the significance of otherness in the study of ethics. He encouraged me to continue asking this question, narrowing it down into a more specific comprehension of humanity. He had taught me simplicity, clarity, and accuracy in writing. He had led me to continue my academic journey with understanding and tolerance in every step of my academic work. Dr. Anne Joh opened my eyes, leading me into the realm of Asian American theology and cross-cultural/contextual theology. She showed me the academic similarity and difference between various ethnic groups in the United States as an Asian American theologian. Dr. Brook Ziporyn had taught me sinology with his philosophical scholarship. He inspired me to compare both traditions, and encouraged me to continue reading Chinese classics in order to develop my academic ability further. Dr. Stephen Ray made me do my academic works more thoroughly and passionately. And Dr. Diane Capitani edited my writing with patience and kindness. As I was writing this, she and I had a meeting every week to review and improve my writing. Lastly, I have to say "thank you so much" to my family. My wife, Sooyoung, had dedicated her life to me, and finally, she accomplished this work through her hands. My sons gave me encouragement whenever I felt academically overwhelmed. As I reach this final goal I can say to them, "I am very happy because of you, my love and my sons."

Introduction

Difference, Otherness and Ethics

ACCORDING TO MARK C. Taylor, "the history of society and culture is a history of the struggle with the endlessly complex problems of difference and otherness."[1] In particular, today is the era of questioning differences and otherness with and against various *isms*, such as communism, totalitarianism, capitalism, racism, and sexism, not only in the realm of politics, but also in the fields of art, psychology, philosophy, theology, and religion. With the sense of the manifestation of otherness, many people describe this period as "postmodern."[2] People have been trying to conceptualize difference and otherness through culture, history, and society. These basic questions of the significance of otherness and difference inspire me to study the ethical manifestation of otherness, namely, the *ethics of otherness*. My argument is that the ethics of otherness is not simply initiated by the reciprocal human relation, but it comes from the acknowledgement and the recognition of the priority of otherness to mutual reciprocity. I will compare Emmanuel Levinas and Confucius (Kongzi) in order to develop my argument.

Whether or not Taylor intends to include the East Asian tradition in his definition of history, his definition is still legitimate for studying both the Euro-American and the East Asian traditions. On the one hand, East Asian religions and philosophies, like Confucianism, Taoism, and Buddhism, focus on human relatedness, harmony, and benevolence *in and for* humanity related to the comprehension of otherness.[3] Harmony and benevolence are the bases of East Asian religion as well as the ethical conceptualization of

---

1. Taylor, *Altarity*, xxi.
2. Ibid.
3. In order to understand East Asian religious tradition, see Fung, *Short History of Chinese Philosophy*.

Introduction

difference and otherness. On the other hand, the question of otherness is the manifestation of human subjectivity in the modern and late modern era in the Euro-American tradition. Euro-American philosophers tend to agree that Descartes's inward turn to the certainty of thinking-self is the starting point for the study of subjectivity. After Descartes, European modern and late modern philosophers have been questioning selfhood, such as Kant's critique of reason, Hegel's all-inclusive system, Kierkegaard's authentic self, Nietzsche's nihilism, Husserl's consciousness, and Heidegger's *Dasein*.[4] These interpretations of selfhood pose the question of otherness in this contemporary postmodern era as society becomes a more multicultural and global community. Humanity asks not only his or her motivation/action, but also the significance of others.

Among these questions of difference and otherness, the main question of this research is about the substance of "who," that is the issue of moral agency, rather than the matters of "what" or "why," related to the issues of moral action(s). Namely, the issue of moral agency is the keystone of this research in terms of the attempt to answer the question: "Who is the doer of this action / these actions?" This question is initiated by the issue of human agency instead of the concept of divine agency. Namely, the issue of moral agency is based on the comprehension of people and their moral actions, rather than a notion of moral sources that come from a divinity or a transcendental being. Based on this preliminary question, I explore the issue of moral agency as concentrating on the study of subjectivity and intersubjectivity. In particular, I explore the significance of intersubjectivity based on my reading of Emmanuel Levinas, and on Confucius (Kongzi) in the primitive Confucian tradition. Interestingly, although there is a huge chronological gap between Levinas and Confucius, about 2,400 years, they share several commonalities, such as their struggles for survival during warring periods, their understandings of human-relatedness, and the valuation of morality and ethics. Levinas started his philosophical study with his experience of the Holocaust. He argued against the limitation of ontology, and emphasized the magnitude of ethics based on his phenomenological discernment of the face of the Other. Confucius (Kongzi) lived during the Spring and Autumn period in ancient China. He criticized the cruelty

---

4. Taylor, *Altarity*, xxi–xxvii. Taylor explains most of these philosophical features in this article, and I added Husserl and Nietzsche. Also, we have to read several ancient philosophical figures in order to comprehend selfhood and otherness, like Aristotle's friendship/politics, and Augustine's idea of love.

INTRODUCTION

of rulers, and tried to develop his own political philosophy based on human relatedness and benevolence (*ren*) in order to build an ideal society.

This book has two goals: a paradigm shift in philosophical studies from Euro-American centered approaches to cross-cultural approaches, and a communicative methodology between these two different traditions. Kwong-loi Shun observes in the comparative philosophy between Chinese (East Asian) and Euro-American that this study has been asymmetrical, that one side proceeds to the other—that is, Euro-American philosophy has tried to interpret Chinese concepts, frameworks, and insights according to a Euro-American philosophical comprehension. Then, he attempts a shift of this asymmetrical comprehension of Chinese philosophy through his comparative study between Euro-American and East Asian, as he argues that Chinese philosophy can illuminate some ethical aspects into the Euro-American tradition in this global community.[5] With these goals, the purpose of this book is not only to interpret Levinas from Kongzi's ethical perspectives, but also to have a creative conversation about otherness and humanness. Hence, I explore their understandings of subjectivity; their appreciation of intersubjectivity or human-relatedness in terms of their assessment of the Other; and their ethical norms for responsibility in Levinas and human-heartedness or benevolence in Kongzi, as I regard the ethical gist of otherness.

Biographical Backgrounds

It is necessary to know about Levinas and Kongzi in order to understand how they developed their philosophical thoughts. Brief biographies of both help us not only grasp the historical backgrounds, but also understand their life struggles that made them inquire of philosophy and ethics. Both philosophers share common ground in their philosophies, in that they experienced extreme life-threatening situations during periods of warfare. They were compelled by these experiences to ask, "What is at stake in humanity?" and they tried to answer this question according to their own philosophical understandings of humanity and culture.

Levinas was born in Lithuania, a colony of Russia, to Jewish parents in 1906. He traveled to Germany in 1929 in order to study philosophy, studied continental philosophies like phenomenology and existentialism, and

5. *Stanford Encyclopedia of Philosophy*, "Comparative Philosophy," citing Shun "Studying Confucian and Comparative Ethics."

Introduction

settled down in France in 1930 to start his professional life. He loved to read Russian authors like Rushkin, Gogol, Dostoyevsky, and Tolstoy, and learned to read the Hebrew Bible and the Talmudic literatures. His experience of the Holocaust made him doubt the significance of phenomenology and ontology, and develop his philosophical thoughts concentrating on ethics. He greatly influenced Western philosophy, as he made philosophers examine the meaning of existence and subjectivity, time and human relation, the importance of language, and the question of God in his works like *Existence and Existents* (1947), *Time and the Other* (1947), *Totality and Infinity* (1961), *Otherwise than Being or Beyond Essence* (1974), and *Of God Who Comes to Mind* (1982).[6] Also, he influenced theology, sociology, literature, linguistics, and others. In particular, the postwar French philosophy is indebted to his phenomenological interpretation of "the other" which became the seed for post-structuralism. After his death in 1995, Derrida eulogized Levinas:

> The question-prayer that turned me toward him perhaps already shared in the experience of the *à-Dieu* is with which I began. The greeting of the *à-Dieu* does not signal the end. "The *à-Dieu* is not a finality," he says, thus challenging the "alternative between being and nothingness," which "is not ultimate." The *à-Dieu* greets the other beyond being, in what is "signified, beyond being, by the word 'glory.'" "The *à-Dieu* is not a process of being: in the call, I am referred back to the other human being through whom this call signifies, to the neighbor for whom I am to fear."[7]

Levinas delved into the significance and signification of being while he experienced the Holocaust. Then, he proposed a new paradigm of philosophy with his account on the face of the Other.

Meanwhile, Kongzi (551–479 BCE) was born and lived during the Spring and Autumn period (722–476 BCE); the *Analects* was collected and edited by his disciples after his death, during the Warring States period (475–221 BCE) of the *Zhou* Dynasty (1100?–249 BCE). The *Zhou* Dynasty had a similar political system to the European feudal system, where the central empire divided their territory into many states. The *Zhou* Dynasty

---

6. Hand, ed., *The Levinas Reader*, 2.

7. Derrida, *Adieu to Emmanuel Levinas*, 13. The direct citation of Derrida is from Levinas's article "Bad Conscience and the Inexorable," in *Face to Face with Levinas*, 35–40. The French word *adieu* means "goodbye," "farewell," or "god-bless," whereas, the etymological meaning of *à-Dieu* is "to God," or "for God." Derrida tried to use both meanings of *adieu* and *à-Dieu*.

Introduction

built an ideal society in the first period (1100?–771 BCE) as it followed the culture of the Sage Kings like Yao, Shun and Yu from the Legendary ages in ancient China. Kongzi praised *Zhou*, noting, "The *Zhou* gazes down upon the two dynasties that preceded it. How brilliant in culture it is! I will follow the *Zhou*."[8] Yet, when the *Zhou* Dynasty was attacked by the barbarian tribes' ally, it had to flee farther east; this is called the Eastern *Zhou* period (770–256 BCE). Ancient China suffered a great deal of life-threatening experiences because each state tried to get power for themselves, fighting each other ceaselessly during the Spring and Autumn period and the Warring States period. Survival was the most important issue during these periods.[9] While Kongzi had lived during the Spring and Autumn period, he explored the great cultural traditions of the Sage Kings and the founders of the *Zhou* Dynasty. The foundation of Kongzi's philosophy is to reevaluate the great traditions of the Sage Kings in ancient China, and to reformulate these traditions into his contemporary society, as he designates himself: "I transmit rather than innovate. I trust in and love the ancient ways."[10] Kongzi developed his philosophy based on his interpretation of *ren* (humanness), and his political thoughts with this conception of *ren*, called *ren*-politics, in order to explore the Way (*tao*) to value humanness for his community and society.

Their experiences of suffering and struggle, thus, led them to examine humanity as the central piece of their philosophical inquiries. Both philosophers started their philosophical studies from their respective philosophical traditions, and found an answer to their questions with different approaches. Levinas questioned the European philosophical traditions, criticized them, and developed his own answer for them. Kongzi reexamined the traditions of the Sage Kings in ancient China, rediscovered the values of them, and tried to transmit them for his contemporaries. Both philosophers valued otherness and human relatedness significantly, explored the manifestation of morality and ethics, and reevaluated humanity as the center of their thoughts of philosophy and religion.

---

8. *Analects*, 23, bk. 3:14. This citation comes from Edward Slingerland's translation of the *Confucius Analects*.

9. See Yao, *Introduction to Confucianism*, and Fung, *Short History of Chinese Philosophy*.

10. *Analects*, 64, bk. 7:1.

Introduction

Structure and Argument

There are four main parts in this book; a theoretical basis on ethics of otherness in the Euro-American tradition, Levinas's interpretation of the face of the Other, Kongzi's comprehension of human relatedness, and a comparison between Levinas and Kongzi. I examine the basic philosophical thoughts of Levinas and Kongzi, discuss how they comprehend otherness and ethics, and how they develop their own ethical thoughts in terms of otherness.

In the first part, I examine the theoretical basis of ethics and otherness as I explore how the Euro-American philosophical tradition interprets reciprocity and human relation as the basis of the ethics of otherness. I explore the philosophical conception of the ethics of otherness in Paul Ricoeur, in particular, his work *Oneself as Another*, in order to study the theoretical bases of the ethics of otherness in the Euro-American tradition. Ricoeur first examines the dialectic of *idem*-identity (sameness) and *ipse*-identity (selfhood), then, he explores the dialectic of selfhood and otherness based on his comprehension of reciprocity as he argues reciprocity is the foundation of the ethics of otherness. Then, he argues Levinas's radical alterity does not fully appreciate the significance of human relation and reciprocity. Richard A. Cohen, however, responds to Ricoeur, as he argues what Levinas values is humanity as moral humanity through the conception of radical otherness. While I examine these arguments between Ricoeur and Cohen, I explore how Ricoeur develops his initial concept of the ethics of otherness in terms of mutual reciprocity, and how Cohen demonstrates a Levinasian approach to radical otherness in order to develop the ethics of otherness. Their arguments reveal to us what are the basic ideas in the ethics of otherness in the Euro-American tradition.

Their arguments of reciprocity and radical otherness are related to my thesis, as I agree with Levinas more than I do with Ricoeur. I examine the foundation on the ethics of otherness in the conception of Levinas's radical otherness rather than mutual reciprocity. Yet, since I found that Levinas's otherness is not fully engaged in otherness, I explore Kongzi's comprehension of human relatedness (*ren*) in order to develop my thesis. Then, I compare both philosophers to examine their commonality and difference, as well as to formulate a creative conversation with each other.

In the second part, I examine Levinas's interpretation of the face of the Other. There are three angles of this study: why Levinas values the face of the Other; how Levinas interprets inter-human relation from his conception of

Introduction

the face; and what is the foundation of Levinas's ethics. For Levinas, the face of the Other is the crux of his philosophy, as he asks the meaning of human existence, which comes from his experience of the Holocaust. He explores the significance of the face, as he demonstrates that the face has the implication of Infinity. In proximity, the face lets people acknowledge his or her responsibility in their inter-human relation. In this sense, human relation is fundamentally asymmetrical rather than reciprocal. This asymmetry formulates the dialectic of selfhood and otherness as it manifests ethics as "first philosophy" rather than ontology. Responsibility, *per se*, is the source of ethics, in that the self has to respond to others according to the summon of the face of the Other in terms of the issues of justice, equality, and peace. In this part, I explore Levinas's phenomenological comprehension of the face, as I examine his interpretation of intersubjectivity or human relation, and the ethical manifestation in his conception of responsibility.

Although Levinas recaptures the ethics of otherness in his thought of the face of the Other and responsibility, he does not fully conceptualize otherness, in that he misses the communal comprehension of human relatedness. With this sense, Kongzi gives us another perspective for the study of the ethics of otherness in his thought of *ren* (humanness/human-relatedness/benevolence). In the third part, thus, I explore Kongzi's main philosophical conception of *ren*. I examine three critical points of Kongzi: how he interprets *ren* in terms of his understanding of humanness; how he comprehends human relation in his thought of *ren* in terms of the idea of the self and the other; and what is the ethical implication in the thought of *ren*. *Ren* is his philosophical foundation, which was unique in ancient China. Kongzi develops his philosophy, in particular in his political thought, based on his conception of *ren*, as he asks about humanness and human relatedness. He also explores how to build an ideal community with his thought of *ren*. He values the Sage Kings traditions in ancient China, in that they made an ideal society with *li* (ritual propriety) and *shu* (understanding of others), which are the foundations of the thought of *ren*. Kongzi examines how people can cultivate themselves according to *ren*, that is, the Way (*tao*) of Virtue (*de*). He develops his unique comprehension of Virtue (capital "V" instead of small "v") in order to illustrate human relatedness. He demonstrates his ethical thought of *ren*, as he values *li* and *shu* as the foundation of community and society. Hence, Kongzi develops his ethical thought of *ren*, as he examines human relatedness as he is actively involved in education and politics in order to show the Way of *ren* for the society.

Introduction

Lastly, I articulate my main argument of the study of the ethics of otherness through my comparative study of Levinas and Kongzi. Again, the ethics of otherness is not simply initiated by the conception of mutual reciprocity; rather, it comes from the acknowledgment and the recognition of the manifestation of otherness. Levinas demonstrates that the dialectic of selfhood and otherness is the foundation of the ethics of otherness. Kongzi articulates that the comprehension of human relatedness is the core of the ethics of otherness. Based on this analysis, I develop my own argument with a twofold approach toward both philosophers: a comprehension of the commonality of both philosophers—how both philosophers value otherness and human relatedness in their ethical thoughts, and a creative conversation of both philosophers—how they can discuss each other in order to find the tenets of the ethics of otherness. The former demonstrates the theoretical basis of the ethics of otherness, and the latter speaks of the practical embodiment of the ethics of otherness. Through this comparative study, I demonstrate my argument that the ethics of otherness is originated by the conception of otherness and human relatedness rather than mutual reciprocity.

Part I

Theoretical Foundation on Ethics and Otherness

RICOEUR HAS A CRITICAL question of otherness and ethics as he values mutual reciprocity and the narrative between the self and the other. Ricoeur initiates his ethical study with the question of "who?" rather than "what?" or "why?" The question of "who?" is not a simple ignorance of the questions of "why?" and "what?" Instead, it comes by the analyses of the replies to these questions.[1] The question of "who?" comes from the interpretation of phenomenological understanding of intention and the ontological events of the autonomous self. Based on this question of moral agency, Ricoeur develops his thoughts of ethics in terms of the dialectic of selfhood and otherness as he analyzes Aristotle's *telos* from the moral action to the agency, and Kant's *aporias* of the deontological events in moral action of the autonomous self. He analyzes the issue of identity first as he distinguishes *idem*-identity and *ipse*-identity.[2] Then, he explores the dialectic of selfhood and otherness as the basis of ethics and morality.

The dialectic of selfhood and sameness formulates the "narrative identity," and this narrative identity has its own ethical implication, in that the authorship of the narratives of the self with the narration of "who I am?" and

---

1. Ricoeur, *Oneself as Another*, 58–61.

2. These are two major meanings of identity which are originated by Latin. *Idem* means "sameness," and *ipse* signifies "selfhood." Ricoeur, *Oneself as Another*, 2–3, explains, "'Same' is used in the context of comparison; its contraries are 'other,' 'contrary,' 'distinct,' 'diverse,' 'unequal,' 'inverse.' The weight of this comparative use of the term 'same' seems so great to me that I shall henceforth take sameness as synonymous with *idem*-identity and shall oppose to it selfhood (*ipseity*), understood as *ipse*-identity."

Part I: Theoretical Foundation on Ethics and Otherness

the answer of "here I am" is based on self-affirmation. The narrative identity determines his or her action according to their predication of "good" and "obligatory," which is the ethical aim of the narrative identity. Ricoeur analyzes the Aristotelian heritage of teleological perspective of "good life," and the Kantian deontological point of "obligation." The predication of "good" and "obligatory" develops a self-designation in terms of "self-esteem" and "self-respect," that is "the most advanced stages of the growth of selfhood."[3] Based on this analysis, Ricoeur explores the significance of mutual reciprocity in the dialectics of selfhood and otherness as his basic conception of the ethics of otherness.

On the one hand, the basic argument in this book is relying on Ricoeur's analysis on human relation and ethics, his interpretation of the dialectic of selfhood and otherness, and his account on the narrative characteristic of human reciprocal relation. On the other hand, it is initiated by a question about the conception of reciprocity in Ricoeur, that is, "can ethics fully ensure the mutual reciprocity in human relation?" Hence, I examine Ricoeur's critique of Levinas in order to explore the ethical implication of human relation. Ricoeur demonstrates self-attestation is the initiative of otherness in terms of ethics as he examines the dialectic of the identity of sameness and selfhood, and the dialectic of selfhood and otherness. He argues Levinas's otherness misses something of the sense of otherness in terms of human relation. Here, I explore Ricoeur's interpretation of selfhood and otherness, the ethical features of otherness, and his critique of Levinas's radical alterity. Then, I explore how Levinas can respond to Ricoeur with Richard A. Cohen's response to Ricoeur's critique of Levinas. I examine what are the foci on otherness and ethics in the Euro-American tradition through these two European philosophers' arguments of subjectivity, intersubjectivity, otherness and ethics through this part.

---

3. Ricoeur, *Oneself as Another*, 170–71.

Chapter 1

Reciprocity and the Radical Otherness

IN THIS FIRST CHAPTER, I will examine Ricoeur's interpretation of ethics of otherness, based on his analysis on the dialectic of selfhood and otherness. I will also see how this dialectic has its own ethical significance. Then, I will explore Ricoeur's critique of Levinas's otherness. Based on this critique of Levinas, I can examine how Ricoeur develops his conception of mutual reciprocity, and how Ricoeur evaluates Levinas's radical alterity. Lastly, I will explore a Levinasian response to Ricoeur, what is the different understanding of human relation between Ricoeur and Levinas. Hence, I will explore the ethical implication of reciprocity, the dialectic of selfhood and otherness, and the narrative identity in human relation in terms of ethics.

The Aim of Ethics and Reciprocity

Ricoeur develops his ethical thought as he delves into the dialectic of selfhood and otherness, exploring the aim of ethics in terms of human relation. Ricoeur's foundation of otherness is developed by the conceptualization of self-esteem and self-respect as the final stage of the growth of selfhood. For Ricoeur, otherness is based on mutual reciprocity, as he examines the tradition of Aristotle's teleology and Kant's deontology. Ricoeur analyzes that ethical aim for "good" in teleological description, related to self-esteem, is prior to the moral norm of "obligatory" in deontological prescription, in terms of self-respect, as he demonstrates that the aim is over the norm.[1] He defines "ethical intention" as "*aiming at the 'good life' with and for other, in*

---

1. Ricoeur, *Oneself as Another*, 171–72.

just institutions."[2] This ethical intention of aiming at the good life develops to the realm of *solicitude* as the reflexive aspect of this aim, which is characterized by self-esteem. This reflectivity of self-esteem proceeds into the sense of the difference between you and I.[3] It makes the self meditate on the other in his or her capacity and realization. Ricoeur illustrates Aristotelian friendship as the epitome of meditation of otherness as it is a transition from the aim of good life to the virtue of human plurality. Friendship is not a psychological feeling of attachment to others at all, but it is an ethical virtue in praxis in order to get the profound idea that "the happy man or woman needs friends." Ricoeur recapitulates, "Otherness, therefore, repossesses the rights that *philautia* appeared to eclipse. It is in connection with the notions of capacity and realization that a place is made for lack, and through the meditation of lack, for *others*."[4] This meditation for others in the dialectic of *philautia* and friendship presents the outcome of otherness as a mutual relationship as the way to "the commonality of 'living together.'"[5]

Kantian morality, as the source of self-respect, is another manifestation of otherness in reciprocity. Categorical imperative, as the *rule of universalization*, does not make a simple confliction between the ethical aim and the moral norm, in that commanding and obeying are situated in the notion of "rational desire" in order to *"live well with and for others in just institutions"* in the praxis to obey by virtue "for satisfying the imperative" as an autonomous self.[6] Ricoeur demonstrates that "when autonomy substitutes for obedience to another obedience to oneself, obedience has lost all character of dependence and submission. True obedience is autonomy," that is, the finalization of self-legislation or *autonomy*.[7] The golden rule, "treat others as you would like them to treat you," exemplifies the dialectic of solicitude and moral imperative as "the enunciation of a *norm of reciprocity*."[8] This sense of the golden rule unfolds the moral norm of "obligation" to value the aim of the "good life" in terms of the dialectic of solicitude. Ricoeur demonstrates the Kantian interpretation of otherness:

2. Ibid., 172.
3. Ibid., 180–81.
4. Ibid., 182. *Philautia* means self-love in Latin.
5. Ibid., 182–83.
6. Ibid., 207–9, 239.
7. Ibid., 210.
8. Ibid., 219.

Reciprocity and the Radical Otherness

The idea of humanity as a singular term is introduced in the context of an abstract universality that governs the principle of autonomy, without the consideration of person. The idea of persons as ends in themselves, however, demands that one take into account the plurality of persons, without allowing one to take this idea as far as the conception of otherness.[9]

Furthermore, this idea of humanity develops into the sense of justice as a moral principle. The rule of reciprocity, thus, amplifies the comprehension of otherness in the foundation of deontology to desire to live *with and for* others.

Based upon this sense of reciprocity, Ricoeur criticizes that Levinas's concept of otherness misses the implication of reciprocity in terms of the issue of human relation. Levinas's account of alterity misses the significance of human relation, in that the priority of the Other and intersubjectivity does not value human relation in the ethical aim of reciprocity. Ricoeur argues:

Levinas's entire philosophy rests on the initiative of the other in the intersubjectivity relation. In reality, this initiative establishes no relation at all, to the extent that the other represents absolute exteriority with respect to an ego defined by the condition of separation. The other, in this sense, absolves himself of any relation. This irrelation defines exteriority as such.[10]

Ricoeur, then, doubts the idea of the face of the Other in Levinas. Ricoeur demonstrates that the face for Levinas "eludes vision, seeming forms, and even eludes hearing, apprehending voices," in that the face does not appear, neither is it a phenomenon, but it is an epiphany. Here, an important question is proposed, "Whose face is it?" which is the issue of irrelation.[11]

Now, the face of the Other "forbids murder and commands justice," as the master who inculcates these ethical modes.[12] This instruction and injunction, however, cannot assure mutual relationship. Instead, "the self is 'summoned to responsibility' by the other."[13] Reciprocity becomes a contrast to the dissymmetry of injunction. The self becomes enjoined in the accusative mode into this dissymmetry of injunction. In this way, "the summons to responsibility has opposite it simply the passivity of an 'I' who

9. Ibid., 222.
10. Ibid., 188–89.
11. Ibid., 189.
12. Ibid.
13. Ibid.

has been called upon."[14] In this sense, the capacity of giving and receiving in the mutual reciprocity loses the resources of the moral *goodness*, in that "a dissymmetry left uncompensated would break off the exchange of giving and receiving and would exclude any instruction by the face within the field of solicitude."[15] With the implication of solicitude, Ricoeur develops his criticism, as he notes that the figure of the master of justice implies the realm of the normative imperative. The aim of ethics, however, does not rely on the formation of norms, but on the matters of conscience, that is, solicitude. Ricoeur argues:

> This is why it is so important to us to give solicitude a more fundamental status that obedience to duty. Its status is that of *benevolent spontaneity*, intimately related to self-esteem within the framework of the aim of the "good" life. On the basis of this benevolent spontaneity, receiving is on an equal footing with the summons to responsibility, in the guise of the self's recognition of the superiority of the authority enjoining it to act in accordance with justice.[16]

Thus, Ricoeur values the superiority of the self as the basis of justice in terms of the issue of equality. Ricoeur criticizes that Levinas's notion of alterity does not guarantee reciprocity at all, but it separates the I from the other, and it makes people *irrelational*.

Critique on the Radical Otherness

Based on this analysis of reciprocity and ethics, Ricoeur develops his criticism on Levinas as he evaluates Levinas's radical otherness. Ricoeur develops his argument of ethics of otherness with his ontological investigation under the hermeneutics of the self. For Ricoeur, on the one hand, ontology implies the *attestation* of the self in the dialectic of sameness and selfhood.[17] The ontological investigation, related to ethics, is based on the reflection and analysis of the dialectic of selfhood and otherness. Ontology, *per se*, relies on its own commitment of the self-attestation. Ontological commitment in self-attestation is affirmed by selfhood "in its difference with

---

14. Ibid.,, 189.
15. Ibid.
16. Ibid., 190.
17. Ibid., introduction.

respect to *sameness* and in its dialectical relation with *otherness*."[18] This attestation is "the assurance—the credence and the trust—of *existing* in the mode of selfhood."[19] Aristotelian *ousia* and its *energeia-dunamis* propose the ground of action of being in *praxis*. This conceptualization of *praxis* discourses with the Heideggerian notion of care (*Sorge*) of being-in-the-world (*Dasein*) in the unity of action in terms of the relation of ontology and otherness.[20]

This ontological discourse relies on phenomenological ontology as "the *phenomenological* respondent to the metacategory of otherness is the variety of experiences of passivity, intertwined in multiple ways in human action."[21] In Ricoeur, "passivity becomes *the* attestation of otherness," in that "the term 'otherness' is reserved for speculative discourse," since two levels of discourse of both phenomenological discourse and ontological discourse are playing each other.[22] This discourse is the way how human beings "account for the work of otherness at the heart of selfhood."[23] With this sense, Ricoeur conceptualizes his idea of modality and passivity of otherness with his hypothesis of "the *triad of passivity and, hence, and of otherness*."[24] The first passivity is embodied by the experience of one's own body, or the flesh, "as the mediator between the self and the world," that takes accordance with his or her practicability and foreignness of others. The second passivity comes from this relation of the self to the foreign, entailed by the sense of the other-self or intersubjectivity. The last passivity, as the most hidden form, is the relation of the self to itself, that is, conscience in the sense of the German *Gewissen*.[25] Ricoeur recaptures this triad of passivity as the following:

---

18. Ibid., 302.
19. Ibid.
20. Ibid., 309–12.
21. Ibid., 318.
22. Ibid.
23. Ibid.
24. Ibid.
25. Ibid. Ricoeur compares *Gewissen* (conscience) with *Bewusstsein* (awareness). The basic idea of the German *Gewissen* is the *suspicion* of "good" and "bad." Ricoeur argues that conscience as suspicion has very complicated ethical implications because it is not only the matter of power and justice, but it is also the issue of the attestation of selfhood and otherness (341).

> By placing conscience in third place in relation to the passivity-otherness of one's own body and to that of other people, we are underscoring the extraordinary complexity and the relational density of the metacategory of otherness. In return, conscience projects after the fact its force of attestation on all the experience of passivity placed before it, inasmuch as conscience is also, through and through, attestation.[26]

Thus, these features of passivity manifest the attestation of otherness in terms of modality.

Ricoeur develops his ethical thoughts of otherness with some more detailed analyses of the passivity and modality of otherness. First, the polarity of body and flesh examines the first idea of the modality of otherness. The self recognizes his or her ego as a flesh, then, they evaluate the body of others while they are living in the world according to their gravity as a living being. This is an ontological reflection of selfhood, that is, ontology of the flesh, in accordance with other concepts of passivity.[27] Second, the otherness of people, as "the metacategory of otherness," is related to the phenomenological hermeneutic of the self, that is, "the relation of the self to the other than self." This is a new dialectic of the Same and the Other, in that "the Other is not only the counterpart of the Same but belongs to the intimate constitution of its sense."[28] This passivity reveals the specific ethical feature in that it makes a shift of the dialectic of self-esteem and friendship to the dialectic of action and affection. This is the shift from the ethical plane of the good to the moral plane of obligation, which are conceptualized in the thoughts of Aristotelian "good" and Kantian "obligatory."[29] Ricoeur argues that the Aristotelian idea of friendship has a sense of "bad" justice in terms of the virtue for others, when the issue of justice occurs in a relation of friendship with others related to the conception of affection. In this sense, the shift from ethics to morality occurs "under the protection of the Golden Rule."[30] In addition, although it is not easy for us to capture the conscience of good and bad with the dialectic of selfhood and otherness, the passivity of conscience illustrates another realm of the

---

26. Ricoeur, *Oneself as Another*, 318–19.

27. Ibid., 319–29.

28. Ibid., 329.

29. Ibid., 330. See also 331–41. Ricoeur also demonstrates the passivity of foreignness as he explores Husserl and Levinas.

30. Ibid., 330.

modality of otherness.[31] Without the moralizing of conscience, the self, as being-enjoined, is conscious of the other with *resoluteness* for others from his or her attestation of themselves.[32] This is the self perception of the Other as an agency, that is, the otherness of conscience.[33] Thus, Ricoeur develops his ethical argument as such, that these conceptualizations of passivity manifest ethics of otherness based on the dialectic of *idem*-identity and *ipse*-identity, and the dialectic of selfhood and otherness.

Ricoeur's critique of Levinas initiates from his interpretation of the second mode of passivity, that is, the relation of the self to the foreign in terms of the affection of the self by the other. Ricoeur's question is "what dialectic of the Same and the Other replies to the demand for a phenomenology of the self *affected* by the other than self."[34] Ricoeur develops his argument as follows:

> It is impossible to construct this dialect in a unilateral manner, whether one attempts, with Husserl, to derive the alter ego from the ego, or whether, with Levinas, one reserves for the Other the exclusive initiative for assigning responsibility to the self.[35]

In particular, Ricoeur criticizes Levinas that there is no place of dialectic between the Same and the Other in Levinas's radical otherness.

Ricoeur points out that Levinas's radical otherness does not come from his negligence of the phenomenological or hermeneutical approach of the dialectic of *idem*-identity and *ipse*-identity, but it does from his interpretation of the *idem*-identity as the central grounds of "an ontology of totality."[36] Then, Ricoeur argues that Levinas's radical otherness "is directed against a conception of the identity of the Same, to which the otherness of the Other is diametrically opposed, but at a level of radicality where the distinction I propose between two sorts of identity, that of *ipse* and the of *idem*, cannot be taken into account."[37] Ricoeur demonstrates that radical otherness becomes the result of the devaluation of "the sense of self-designation"

---

31. Ibid., 341–42.
32. Ibid., 350.
33. Ibid., 354.
34. Ibid., 331.
35. Ibid.
36. Ibid., 335.
37. Ibid.

as the root of "discourse, action, narrative, or ethical commitment."[38] This state of separation of these two identities makes otherness "the equivalent of radical exteriority."[39] More seriously, Levinas's radical alterity becomes idealistic and solipsistic, as Ricoeur notes that "to represent something to oneself is to assimilate it to oneself, to include it in oneself, and hence to deny its otherness."[40]

Ricoeur develops his criticism of Levinas with three focal analyses of the absolute otherness as he posits that Levinas's radical otherness is "the use of *hyperbole*," that is, "the hyperbole of separation" between the Same and the Other.[41] The first hyperbole is "the *epiphany* of the face." The "evincing" of the face does not value the visual form, nor the hearing of voices. The Other is not the interlocutor any longer: instead, he or she becomes "a paradigmatic figure of the type of a master of justice," that is, a teaching rather than interlocution.[42] This is the hyperbole of "Elevation" and "Exteriority," as the former "summons me as though from Sinai," and the latter "awakens no reminiscence." Ricoeur continues:

> Since the initiative belongs wholly to the Other, it is in the accusative—a mode well named—that the I is met by the injunction and made capable of answering, again in the accusative: "It's me here!" Hyperbole culminates in the affirmation that the teaching of the face reestablishes no primacy of relation with respect to the terms. No middle ground, no between, is secured to lessen the utter dissymmetry between the Same and the Other.[43]

Ricoeur points out that this hyperbolic comprehension of the face of the Other mainly appears within the conceptualization of asymmetry of human relationship in *Totality and Infinity*.

Ricoeur demonstrates another hyperbolic feature in Levinas's interpretation of responsibility as "paroxysm," as Ricoeur notes that Levinas's responsibility is "the *assignment of responsibility*," which is mainly employed in *Otherwise than Being or Beyond Essence*.[44] The assignment of responsibility is the injunction which is prior to any beginning, that

38. Ibid.,, 335.
39. Ibid., 336.
40. Ibid.
41. Ibid., 337.
42. Ibid.
43. Ibid., 337–38.
44. Ibid., 338.

is, *an-archy*. Here, Levinas reaches a paroxysm of substitution of the self for the Other, as Levinas argues, "under accusation by everyone, the responsibility for everyone goes to the point of substitution. A subject is a hostage."[45] Ricoeur disagrees with this statement, as he notes, "this expression, the most excessive of all, is thrown out here in order to prevent the insidious return of the self-affirmation of some 'clandestine and hidden freedom' maintained even within the passivity of the self summoned to responsibility."[46] Ricoeur recapitulates that "the Other is no longer the master of justice here, but the offender, who, as an offender, no less requires the gesture of pardon and expiration."[47] Substitution is the excessive examination of the expiration of the unity of identity and alterity, because the relation of otherness and identity becomes hollowed into the abyss through this process of substitution.[48]

This paroxysm of substitution, Ricoeur argues, is "*the* hyperbole of separation," in that separation does not only lead me to the "hyperbole of exteriority" on "the side of the Same," but it also leads me to "an impasse" on "the side of the other."[49] In this sense of separation, the self cannot have any capacity of reception which is able to reconsider, discern, recognize and take into account on the otherness within this reflective structure.[50] Ricoeur asks his fundamental questions about the conception of substitution in Levinas:

> Finally, to meditate the opening of the Same onto the Other and the internalization of the voice of the Other in the Same, must not language contribute its resources of communication, hence of reciprocity, as is attested by the exchange of personal pronouns mentioned so many times in the preceding studies, an exchange that reflects a more radical one, that of question and answer in which the roles are continually reversed? In short, is it not necessary that a dialogue superpose a relation on the supposedly absolute distance between the separate I and the teaching Other?[51]

---

45. Ibid. This direct citation in Ricoeur is from Levinas, *Otherwise than Being*, 112.
46. Ricoeur, *Oneself as Another*, 338.
47. Ibid.
48. Ibid.
49. Ibid., 339 (italics mine).
50. Ibid.
51. Ibid.

For Ricoeur, thus, the conception of substitution exemplifies the hyperbole of separation between the self and the other without any assurance of human relation or mutual reciprocity.

Lastly, Ricoeur asks to Levinas: "Who is obsessed by the Other? Who is hostage to the Other if not a Same no longer defined by separation but my its contrary, Substitution?"[52] Ricoeur analyzes these questions with the significance of testimony. If the Self does not testify to the idea of the assignment of responsibility and the injunction of the Other, nothing testifies to these matters because the testimony is given to "the glory of the infinite," as the manifestation of the absolute, the Elevated, and the Exteriority.[53] In this sense, Ricoeur argues that Levinas misses the attestation of the self, which is the basis of the conceptualization of otherness:

> To be sure, Levinas never speaks of the attestation *of self*, the very expression being suspected of leading back to the "certainty of the ego." It remains that, through the form of the accusative, the first person is indirectly involved and that the accusative cannot remain "nonassumable," to borrow an expression quoted above, under pain of stripping all meaning from the very theme of substitution, under the aegis of which Levinas reassumes the theme of testimony.[54]

Thus, substitution culminates in Levinas's hyperbole of the radical alterity, in that it signifies "the most total passivity" without any sense of the self-attestation.[55] Paradoxically, the ethical source of injunction and responsibility for the Other is diminished in this hyperbolic sense of the radical alterity.[56]

Levinasian Response to Ricoeur

Richard A. Cohen responds to Ricoeur's critique of Levinas with his Levinasian interpretation of ethics and otherness, as he analyzes Ricoeur's ethical interpretation of selfhood and otherness. Cohen examines Ricoeur's basic phrase on ethics, "as aims at the 'good life' with and for others, in just institutions." According to Cohen, there are three foci in this phrase:

52. Ibid., , 340.
53. Ibid.
54. Ibid.
55. Ibid.
56. Ibid., 341.

Reciprocity and the Radical Otherness

"the self as moral character" in the phrase of "aiming at the good life"; "the alterity of moral sociality" in "with and for other"; and "the reconciliation of moral self and others as justice" in "in just institution."[57] After pointing out these foci, Cohen argues:

> The differences separating Ricoeur and Levinas are sharp. First, Ricoeur's hierarchy of self and other is exactly the reverse of Levinas's, for whom moral sociality precedes moral character. Second, Ricoeur equates moral sociality with normativity. For Levinas, in contrast, moral sociality does not by itself, or does not at first manifest itself as normativity. Normativity, for Levinas, is a conditioned development which appears later or consequent at the level of justice.[58]

Cohen demonstrates that Levinas's initial morality on sociality is "purer or more stringent than normativity," which means "laws are a part of a developed morality, but they are not its initial moment."[59] Within this sense, Levinas's basis of morality is different from Ricoeur, in particular, not only from the Kantian implication of moral norms, but also from the normative comprehension of the Aristotelian concept of mutual reciprocity in Ricoeur.[60]

What Levinas discerns is not the excessive exteriority of others, nor the extreme passivity or separation of the self, which causes the "irrelation" between the self and the other. Nor is it the *benevolent spontaneity* on the exchange of *giving and receiving* human relation in terms of ethical actions.[61] Instead, what Levinas raises is "the priority of the encounter with the alterity of the other, ethical priority, to the statue of the very humanity of the human."[62] For Levinas, "humanity and moral humanity arise together," which means morality is not prior to humanity, but it emerges from humanity.[63] Therefore,

> the only genuine other is the commanding-obliging other, the moral other. This level, Levinas would argue, must be presupposed by any analysis of hermeneutics of moral life. Without it

---

57. Cohen, "Moral Selfhood," in Cohen and Marsh, *Ricoeur as Another*, 128.
58. Ibid., 129.
59. Ibid.
60. Ibid., 129–30.
61. Ibid., 131–32.
62. Ibid., 131.
63. Ibid., 133–34.

> one could not even begin to speak of such things as the goodness of the "good life," or the benevolence of spontaneity. . . . The superiority of the other in an exchange of giving and receiving cannot be called moral, rather than simply economic, unless the moral dimension as such is already operative through a prior encounter with alterity as such.[64]

For Levinas, the moral self is formulated by the irreplaceable subjection to the other, as "elected" by the other. The "I," no one but myself, is responsible in the face of the Other. Within this sense of responsibility, the "I" can become the genuine self for *the other* through his or her life, as the "unrelating relation," that is, the abiding status of humanity as moral humanity.[65]

Cohen responds more specifically to Ricoeur's ontological elucidation of ethics and otherness. Cohen points out the different comprehension of Heidegger in both Ricoeur and Levinas. Both philosophers start their ethical argument on ontology from Heidegger in terms of conscience and solicitude of the self as they read Heidegger critically. Their philosophical outcomes from Heidegger, however, are completely different. In spite of his disagreement with the results of Heidegger's "moral deficiency of Dasein," Ricoeur follows Heideggerian methodology on the history of philosophy as he values the "moral reconstruction of Dasein's conscience."[66] With this notion on Heidegger, Ricoeur criticizes that the radical otherness misconceptualizes human relation, introduces *hyperbole* on otherness and selfhood, and proposes an alternative hypothesis of selfhood as "being-enjoined."[67] On the contrary, Levinas dissents from both the results of Dasein's morality and the philosophical methodology in Heidegger, but Levinas emphasizes ethics rather than Heideggerian ontology.[68]

Besides the ethical encounter of the Other in human relation, Cohen points out several more features of human relation in Levinas: familial dimension of selfhood, receptivity of others, and ethical testimony of the Other. Ricoeur disregards the familial dimension of selfhood of Levinas in *Totality and Infinity*, which is one of the basic concepts of human relation. This familial dimension of selfhood comes from sexuality and fecundity as

---

64. Cohen, "Moral Selfhood," 134.
65. Ibid. Cohen's citation of Levinas comes from *Totality and Infinity*, 295.
66. Cohen, "Moral Selfhood," 135–36.
67. Ibid., 137.
68. Ibid.

the original form of human relation.⁶⁹ Then, Cohen argues that Ricoeur's claim of the separation of the self in Levinas is not legitimate, in that Levinas does not fall into the solipsistic abyss of the Cartesian ego, but he intends a reorientation of philosophy from its epistemological base to the ethical height. In this sense, receptivity in Levinas is not characterized as "benevolent spontaneity." Instead, again, what Levinas counts on is not "the relation *between* self and other," but "the encounter with alterity as transcendence, as the outside, the other," that is, the reorientation of the epistemological framework in human subjectivity.⁷⁰ Therefore, the testimony of the Other, as the conceptualization of substitution of the self to the Other, is not the reversal of the self to the other within the recognition of the superiority of the other. It is the testimony of revelation of the Infinite, as it testifies "of and for the other's moral height," that is, alterity.⁷¹ Truly, it does not concern Ricoeur's moral righteousness of the self within the *conatus* of self-attestation. Rather, it is the conatus of the self in order to be humbled "for-the-other."⁷² This is Levinas's philosophical project: to interpret what is at stake in Western ontology and how significant ethics is instead of ontology through his comprehension of humanity and human morality. Cohen recapitulates, "Ricoeur can never come across this totality precisely because all his investigations operate within it, unwittingly conforming to its contours. Levinas's thought, in contrast, articulates this totality by exceeding and rupturing it—from a moral angle, a height."⁷³

The sense of hyperbole of Ricoeur is also caused by the misconception of Levinasian interpretation of morality and justice. Levinas distinguishes the morality of the face of the Other and the normative demands of justice. Cohen exemplifies Richard Weaver's explanation of exaggeration as caricature and exaggeration as prophecy, in *The Ethics of Rhetoric*, in order to value Levinas's sense of the excess of morality as "moral."⁷⁴ Since the rhetoric of prophets in the biblical tradition contained truth in order that a persuasion could be possible, the excessive rhetoric of Levinas is not a

69. Ibid., 138–39.
70. Ibid., 140–42.
71. Ibid., 146.
72. Ibid., 144.
73. Ibid., 147.
74. Ibid., 150–51.

meaningless caricature, but a prophecy which includes truth of morality and humanity. What Levinas attempts is

> to articulate neither being nor non-being, nor becoming, but rather a "real potentiality or possible actuality," the priority of goodness over being, and the insatiable desire of the self that respond to this call. To do so he must be a "noble rhetorician," not because moral exigency, and the exhortative language it puts into play, is a gloss on being, a decoration or luxury, but because morality makes greater demands than being, cuts deeper than being.[75]

Here, the significance of Levinas's ethics is to highlight morality itself. Cohen articulates, "The human is not the measure, but is measured by morality."[76] Therefore, the "philosophical reflection in general" for Levinas is the "moral reflection" of the self, and the rhetorical exaggeration comes from this moral reflection rather than any sense of hyperbole.[77] Cohen, thus, responds to Ricoeur as he notes that Levinas's alterity comes from the different elucidation of the selfhood and otherness with Ricoeur's comprehension of otherness.

Here, Ricoeur and Levinas show the main issues of the ethical study of selfhood and otherness in the Euro-American tradition, in particular, in the modern, late modern, and postmodern tradition, such as the issues of identity, human relation, and ethical aims. Ricoeur appreciates otherness with the dialectic of *idem*-identity and *ipse*-identity, and the dialectic of selfhood and otherness. Then, Ricoeur develops his ethical thought as he values the Aristotelian concept of "good," in terms of the issue of agency, and the Kantian notion of "obligatory," of the autonomous self, with the ethical significance of these traditions. Ethics comes from the self-attestation for "good" and "obligatory" through the process of manifestation of selfhood and otherness. With this sense, Ricoeur criticizes Levinas's radical otherness as it is hyperbolic and irrelational, in that it overexpresses the Other and separates the self from others. According to Ricoeur, these features in Levinas's radical alterity do not clearly grasp the significance of the *attestation of self* in terms of the manifestation of otherness. On the contrary, Richard A. Cohen responds to Ricoeur as he points out that Levinasian ethics is based on humanity and human morality which values otherness in order to explore the morality of the

75. Ibid., 152.
76. Ibid.
77. Ibid., 153.

self. These interpretations of otherness between Ricoeur and Levinas demonstrate the Euro-American comprehension of otherness and ethics. Through these interpretations, as I discussed above, I agree with Levinas's radical otherness for the study of the ethics of otherness. In the next chapter, thus, I will explore Levinas's account on otherness as I examine the significance of the face of the Other, and responsibility of the self in the dialectic of selfhood and otherness.

Part II

Emmanuel Levinas

The Face of the Other, Intersubjectivity, and Ethics

LEVINAS ACCOUNTS ON THE face of the Other, inter-human relation in his ethical thought as his basic philosophical argument. Levinas endeavors to analyze experiences among humans, in particular, the Holocaust, as the center of philosophy rather than the scrutiny of the universal truths.[1] Levinas initiates his philosophical journey from his phenomenological interpretation of the face of the Other. The face of the Other is the sources of Infinity, inter-human relation, and ethics. In this part, I will explore how Levinas interprets the face of the Other, how Levinas illustrates inter-human relation, and how Levinas develops his ethical thoughts.

Levinas initiates his philosophical works form Husserl and Heidegger.[2] Husserl starts his philosophical journey with his famous slogan, "back to the things themselves," instead of the pure *cogito*.[3] Husserl questions the meaning of the doubting-self, and then asks what we have really experienced in the world. Husserl delves into the consciousness of the self, the intentionality of the self, the transcendental egos, and intuition. He develops phenomenology that concentrates on the phenomenon of the available mode of the presentation of essences rather than the distinct

---

1. Hand, ed., *The Levinas Reader*, , 2.

2. Davis, "Phenomenology," in *Levinas: An Introduction*, 10–16. According to Davis, after Levinas fully understands the work of Husserl, Levinas criticized Husserl, noting that Husserlian phenomenology is lacking the interpretation of historicity, following into intellectualism in that it made an abstraction of consciousness from history.

3. Ibid., 10–11.

Part II: Emmanuel Levinas

form of essences.[4] Heidegger renews Husserl's phenomenology in his phenomenological ontology with the question of Being. Heidegger tries to synthesize both the matter of ontology and the descriptive experience. His critical term, *Dasein*, comes from the phenomenological considerations of the disclosedness, thrownness and projection of existence into the world.[5] *Desein*'s Being cannot be separated from the temporality and historicity. With this sense, Heidegger criticizes Husserlian phenomenology and its missing concept of historicity, and then he develops his ontological understanding with the synthesis of phenomenology and ontology.[6]

Both philosophers' thoughts of the self and the other become the basic philosophical questions for Levinas. According to Husserl, the transcendental Egos cannot meet the other directly, so the egos meet the other as he or she reflects the behaviors of the other with empathy, and they respect the similarity of the other as their own selves. This is the space where Husserlian intersubjectivity occurs, such that the ego encounters and supports the other with harmony, the sense of community, and reciprocity. Heidegger criticizes Husserl's interpretation of intersubjectivity as such that it is a simple reflection of the self toward the other, since there is no place *for* the other in Husserl's thought of the self. Heidegger rejects the notion of the empathy of Husserl since the other in Husserl is a mere duplication of the self. Heidegger proposes his ontological interpretation of *Mitsein* (Being-with), arguing that *Dasein* exists *with* other in the world. Heidegger values the presence of others as much as *Desein* dwells in the world. As *Dasein* exists *with* the other, the existence of the other can obtain the ontical significance.[7]

Levinas's basic question originates from the elucidation of the other of both philosophers. Levinas opposes not only Husserl's concept of empathy/consciousness of the transcendental Egos, but also Heidegger's conception of *Dasein/Mitsein*. To Levinas, both prioritize the self, objectify the other, and totalize humanity. The Other is not another self, nor the relationship of *Dasein* with the world. Rather, the Other is an essential mystery as the self experiences an enigmatic encounter with the Other. Levinas criticizes that

---

4. Ibid.

5. The literal meaning of the German word, *Dasein*, is being(sein)-there(da). *Dasein* is situated both in time and space with temporality and historicity. English translators usually use this term, *Dasein*, as itself because of this philosophical meaning.

6. Davis, "Phenomenology," 14–17.

7. Ibid., 25–30.

both philosophers' phenomenology fails to think of the Other as Other.[8] The mysterious encounter of the self with the Other makes Levinas think of the limitation of Western ontology and phenomenology. Consequently, Levinas argues that ethics is the "first philosophy" rather than ontology because ethics can respond to this enigmatic existence of the Other.

Based on these philosophical arguments in Levinas, I will explore the phenomenological understanding of the face of the Other, the comprehension of ipseity (selfhood) and alterity (otherness) in terms of the interpretation of intersubjectivity, the concept of responsibility, and the ethics of otherness in Levinas. First, I will examine the reason why Levinas initiates his philosophical journey from his phenomenological interpretation of the face of the Other, and what is the philosophical manifestation of the face of the Other. My second exploration is how he comprehends human subjectivity and intersubjectivity, and why otherness is significant in human relations. And the last point is how otherness formulates its ethical implication, and how Levinas values responsibility as his key conception of ethics. Hence, I will examine the dialectic of selfhood and otherness in Levinas in order to explore one of the basic tenets in the ethics of otherness in this part.

---

8. Ibid., 30–33.

Chapter 2

The Face of the Other

LEVINAS STARTS HIS PHILOSOPHICAL inquiry from his skepticism of European ontology. Then, Levinas does not only contemplate the phenomenality of the face of the Other, but he also explores the trace of the face of the Other. I will examine how Levinas explores the phenomenality and the trace of the face of the Other, and how Levinas develops his philosophical thoughts through his interpretation of the face of the Other in this chapter.

Why Face?

In 1951, Levinas published an essay, "Is Ontology Fundamental," proposing two rudimental questions on ontology: "Does not the primacy of ontology among the branches of knowledge rest on a most obvious evidence? Does not all knowledge of relations by which beings are connected or opposed to one another already involve the comprehension of the fact that these relations and these beings exist?"[1] These questions tell us about the foundational philosophical concerns of Levinas, which were initiated by Levinas's experience of the Holocaust, that is, the extreme experience of the possibility of total negation of beings. Levinas demonstrates this war period as "the Evil of all time," because of the hatred and contempt, and the dread of destitution and destruction among beings.[2] He depicts a serious picture of this period:

---

1. Levinas, "Is Ontology Fundamental?," in *Basic Philosophical Writings*, 2. We can also read this article in a different translation in *Entre Nous*, 1–11.
2. Levinas, "Nameless," in *Proper Names*, 119.

Interregnum or end of the Institutions, or as if being itself had been suspended. Nothing was official anymore. Nothing was objective. Not the least manifesto on the rights of Man. No "leftist intellectual protest"! Absence of any homeland, eviction from all French soil! Silence of every Church! Insecurity of all companionship. So these were "the straits" of the first chapter of Lamentations: "None to comfort her!", and the complaint of the Kippur ritual: "No high priest to offer sacrifices, nor any altar on which to place our holocausts!"[3]

He demonstrates this theme in the dedication of his book *Otherwise than Being or Beyond Essence*, where he writes sparingly that his philosophical concerns are based on his experience of the Holocaust: "To the memory of those who were closest among the six million assassinated by the National Socialists, and of the millions on millions of all confessions and all nations, victims of the same hatred of the other man, the same anti-semitism."[4] Levinas constantly ruminates on the horror of the massacre of the Holocaust. In particular, he takes up the issue of totalitarianism much more seriously than other political regimes, as he asks what is at stake *in and between* people, and where humanity goes *under and through* this horrible experience of the Holocaust.

Levinas turns to Heideggerian phenomenological ontology in order to find answers to these questions. Levinas points out that the basic features in Heideggerian ontology, such as authenticity, facticity, comportment, comprehension, and temporality of being, have a very ambiguous connotation in that *Dasein* (Being-there) engages in the world like a "dramatic event of being-in-the-world" without any philosophical elucidations of existence.[5] Levinas clarifies this point, noting that "the philosophy of existence immediately effaces itself before ontology."[6] Then, Levinas evaluates Heidegger's comprehension of openness of *Dasein* to the world. This openness can comprehend the relation between subject and the other, or the relation between subject and object, that is, being-with-the-other (*Mitsein*).[7] Levinas asks whether or not relation with the other is the matter of *letting be* in this

---

3. Ibid., 119–20.
4. Levinas, *Otherwise than Being*, dedication.
5. Levinas, "Is Ontology Fundamental," 3–4.
6. Ibid.
7. Ibid., 6.

The Face of the Other

comprehension of the ontological relation.[8] If the matter of this ontological relation is a simple *letting be*, the process of letting be is not a full comprehension of relation because it becomes the process of objectification of the other. Instead, Levinas analyzes human relations with both implications of *letting-be* and *accepted-by*, in that "to comprehend a person is already to speak with him."[9] This is the invocation of the other as interlocutor. It is impossible for a person to encounter the other without speaking, that is, the comprehension of being is the expression of a person with the other. At this point, the comprehension of a relation is not based on the knowledge of the other, but it is constituted by the institution of the social relation among people. Therefore, the relation with the other is not ontology at all.[10] Rather:

> This tie to the other, which does not reduce itself to the representation of the Other but rather to his invocation, where invocation is not preceded by comprehension, we call *religion*. The essence of discourse is prayer. What distinguishes thought aiming at an object from the tie with a person is that the latter is articulated in the vocative: what is named is at the same time that which is called.[11]

The term *religion* in Levinas is not about God or the sacred. Nor is it about the exercise of power. Instead, it is human relation in terms of the Infinite in human face, as follows:

> The concept of contemporary philosophy to liberate human beings from the categories adapted uniquely for things cannot therefore content itself with notions of dynamism, duration, transcendence, or freedom, as opposed to those of the static, the inert, the determined, as a description of the human essence. In order to say what is human nature, it is not so much a matter of opposing on essence to another. It is above all a matter of finding a place where the human no longer concerns us from the perspective of the horizon of being, that is to say, no longer offers itself to our powers. A being as such (and not as incarnation of universal being) can only be in a relation where we speak to this being. A being is a human being and it is as a neighbor that a human being is accessible—as a face.[12]

---

8. Ibid. (italics original).
9. Ibid.
10. Ibid., 7.
11. Ibid., 7–8.
12. Ibid., 8. Derrida points out this philosophical feature of infinity as a terminology, i.e., "metaphysical transcendence," in his article "Violence and Metaphysics," in Katz, *Emmanuel Levinas*, 1:88–173 (the original source is from Derrida, *Writing and*

Part II: Emmanuel Levinas

Adriaan Peperzak explains that the idea of the infinite "*thinks more than it thinks*. In this manner, the infinite shows its exteriority, its transcendence, and its radical highness." According to Peperzak, the idea of the infinite is not the matter of an all-embracing universality but it is the absolute alterity.[13]

Here, Levinas analyzes "the impossible possibility" of the temptation of the total negation of beings because of the presence of the face.[14] The relation with the other face to face makes beings unable to kill, because the relation with the other is based on the situation of discourse.[15] The Other is the being whom a person wishes to kill, that is, the total negation. This power seems to let a person have a triumphant moment as he or she can wish to kill the other. At this moment, however, the realization of this power also makes a person recognize that the other has escaped from his or her power, in that the encounter of the face of the other speaks to oneself. When a person does not have to look at the face of the other, he or she might feel their power. The presence of the face, however, shows the impossible possibility of murder in that the face speaks in itself.[16] This is the signification of the face of the Other in terms of the relation of human beings:

> That the relation with a *being* is the invocation of a face and already speech, a relation with a certain depth rather than with a horizon—a breach in the horizon—that my neighbor is the being par excellence, can indeed appear somewhat surprising when one is accustomed to the conception of a being that is by itself insignificant, a profile against a luminous horizon and only acquiring signification in virtue of its presence within this horizon. The face *signifies* otherwise. In it the infinite resistance of a being to our

---

Difference, 79–153). Derrida writes, "The absolute overflowing of ontology—as the totality and unity of the same: Being—by the other occurs as infinity because no totality can constrain it. The infinity irreducible to the *representation* of infinity, the infinity exceeding the ideation in which it is thought, thought of as more than I can think, as the which cannot be an object or a simple 'objective reality' of the idea—such is the pole of metaphysical transcendence. After the *epekeina tes ousias*, the Cartesian idea of infinity made metaphysics emerge for a second time in Western ontology. But what neither Plato nor Descartes recognized is that the expression of this infinity is the *face*."

"*Epekeina tes ousias*" means "beyond beingness," in Greek. "*Epekeina tes ousias*" is a phrase from Plato's *Republic* 509b.

13. Peperzak, *To the Other*, 59.

14. I use this term "impossible possibility" with the literal meaning in general. Yet, I borrowed this term "impossible possibility" from Reinhold Niebuhr's works, in particular, from his works *Interpretation of Christian Ethics* and *Moral Man and Immoral Society*.

15. Levinas, "Is Ontology Fundamental," 9.

16. Ibid.

power affirms itself precisely against the murderous will that it defies; because, completely naked (and the nakedness of the face is not a figure of style), the face signifies itself.[17]

Then, Levinas concludes that "the human only lends itself to a relation that is not a power" in his article "Is Ontology Fundamental."[18] Levinas answers his philosophical questions, such that philosophical research is not a simple reflection on the self or existence, but it is the narrative of the adventure of being through the relation and the experience to the realms of the infinite.[19] The face is not only the departure of this journey, but it is also the destination of it. Levinas has kept this journey to encounter the face in his philosophical works, especially in *Totality and Infinity* in terms of the significance and signification of the face, and in *Otherwise than Being or Beyond Essence* related to the trace and proximity of the face.

The Phenomenality of the Face: Infinity

Levinas develops his argument that the other's face has an unconditional character in itself, that is Infinity, as he uses the religious term *revelation*, and *epiphany*, based on his phenomenological comprehension of the exteriority of the face. Levinas delves into the implication of the same, related to totality in Western philosophy, especially in ontology, as we discussed above. Then, he emphasizes the infinity of the other based on his ontological and phenomenological analysis of the Other. In Levinas, totality is "the reign of the same" between the self and the other, that is, "everything and everybody exists as part of a whole or as case under a law."[20] Levinas criticizes Heideggerian ontology severely as "ontology as first philosophy is a philosophy of power," as it secures the totality of the State with the pretext of Truth and Universality which makes human being impersonal and inhumane.[21] Levinas argues:

> The "egoism" of ontology is maintained even when, denouncing Socratic philosophy as already forgetful of Being and already on

---

17. Ibid., 10.
18. Ibid.
19. Ibid.
20. Waldenfels, "Levinas and the Face of the Other," in Critchley and Bernasconi, *Cambridge Companion to Levinas*, 66.
21. Levinas, *Totality and Infinity*, 46.

> the way to the notion of the "subject" and technological power, Heidegger finds in Presocratism thought as obedience to the truth of Being. This obedience would be accomplished in existing as builder and cultivator, effecting the unity of the site which sustain space.... Ontology becomes ontology of nature, impersonal fecundity, faceless generous mother, matrix of particular beings, inexhaustible matter for things.[22]

Totalitarian regimes utilize this philosophy of power in order to manipulate people under tyrannical oppression, which enslaves humanity to the totalitarian rulers without any sense of freedom and justice. Totality, *per se*, builds its foundation on violence. Consequently, ceaseless wars occur as the enrooted form of enslavement for this philosophy of power.[23] By contrast, the infinity of the other precedes totality, in that otherness can overcome the limitation of any orders of violence, the tyrannical oppression.[24] To break totality is to set "a central role" of the face of the Other in the interpretation of existence rather than the philosophy of power.[25]

The "central role" of the face does not question "what does 'face' mean?" Rather, it does not try to define anything at all. The face has no "plastic" form which can be transformed into an image.[26] Instead, "the face speaks" to us as an interlocutor. The face is not manifested by any form or definition that expresses itself as a "living presence." Levinas demonstrates that "the life of expression consists in undoing the form in which the existent, exposed as a theme, is thereby dissimulated.... The manifestation of the face is already discourse."[27] The signification of oneself, thus, is not the acceptable formation to the Same, but it is "the presence of exteriority" in terms of discourse. Signification and expression are not intellectual intuition any longer, but they are "the production of meaning," which comes from the frankness and welcoming of the Other while discourse occurs.[28] This is the request to recognize the relationship with the Other based on relational language, the interpellation and the invocation. The face of the

---

22. Ibid.
23. Ibid., 46–47.
24. Waldenfels, "Levinas and the Face of the Other," in Critchley and Bernasconi, *Cambridge Companion to Levinas*, 66.
25. Ibid.
26. Ibid., 66–67.
27. Levinas, *Totality and Infinity*, 66.
28. Ibid., 66–67.

The Face of the Other

Other seems not to have any quiddity,[29] but the interpellation of the Other makes the I see the Other as "the respected," that is, the acknowledgment of the heterogeneity of the I which is confirmed and maintained by the relationship between the I and the Other.[30] Thus, the face signifies the existence of humanity through the discourse between people as it expresses the presence of Being.

The face of the Other is also related to the issue of truth and justice. The presence of existence and the interpellation speak incessantly of their gravity of assistance for them, that is, the process of actualization and objectification of speech. This expression of the presence of the face manifests a master in this process of actualization and objectification of the face, as the Other is welcomed as an interlocutor. That is the exteriority of the face which is established by language in terms of transcendence.[31] The I can not only understand the signification of the face of the Other through the expression, the language, but also envision the Other as the Other following the issue of truth and justice. Levinas elaborates:

> *The other qua other is the Other*. To "let him be" the relationship of discourse is required; pure "disclosure," where he is proposed as a theme, does not respect him enough for that. *We call justice this face to face approach, in conversation*. If truth arises in the absolute *experience* in which being gleams with its own light, then truth is produced only in veritable conversation of in justice.[32]

---

29. There is an interesting observation of Levinas related to this matter of quiddity in his early work *Time and the Other*, published in 1947. Levinas describes the face-to-face relationship as so assumptive that "the relationship with the Other, the face-to-face with the Other, the encounter with a face that at once gives and conceals the Other, is the situation in which an event happens to a subject who does not assume it. Who is utterly unable in its regard, but where nonetheless in a certain way it is in front of the subject. The other 'assumed' is the Other."

30. Levinas, *Totality and Infinity*, 69.

31. Ibid., 69–70.

32. Ibid., 71. The first sentence of this citation, in French, is "*L'Autre en tant qu'autre est Autrui*." According to the note of translator of *Totality and Infinity*, the translation of *l'Autre* and *Autrui* is not doable enough in English. So, Lingis writes a note: "With the author's permission, we are translating '*autrui*' (the personal Other, the you) by 'Other,' and '*autre*' by 'other.' In doing so, we regrettably sacrifice the possibility of reproducing the author's use of capital or small letters with both these terms in the French text" (*Totality and Infinity*, 24–25). Here is another translator's note in *Basic Philosophical Writing*, xvi–xv: "In order to indicate the difference between *l'autre* and *autrui*, both of which we translate as 'the other' (or 'the Other'), we have added between parentheses *autrui* when that is the word used in the French text. However, there are a few places where this

Levinas explains that "truth is made by relation with the Other our master," because "society does not proceed from the contemplation of the true."[33] The issue of justice brings its voice into this reality of humanity and society:

> Truth is thus bound up with the social relation, which is justice. Justice consists in recognizing in the Other my master. Equality among persons means nothing of itself; it has an economic meaning and presupposes money, and already rests on justice—which, when well-ordered, beings with the Other. Justice is the recognition of his privilege qua Other and his mastery, is access to the Other outside of rhetoric, which is ruse, emprise, and exploitation. And in this sense justice coincides with the overcoming of rhetoric.[34]

The exteriority of the face is the basis of human relationship and the recognition of a mastery. My freedom is restricted by a master, in that only this master authorizes my action,[35] and he or she opposes me, not in its manifestation, but in its way of being, that is, ontological opposition.[36] This opposition, however, is not a simple negation of my freedom, but it is prior to my freedom, paradoxically, which puts my freedom into action.[37] Thus, the face of the Other is not only the source of justice (it is not a case of a just action),[38] but it also is the foundation of truth which makes "the sovereign exercise of freedom possible."[39]

Levinas's sketch of the face of the Other and the linguistic relationship between the I and the Other depicts the transcendental image of the face as the revelation and epiphany of the face. The epiphany of the face is not a perception of the way that a person appears to another, but it is the summon of the Other against one's own power or possession.[40] Levinas

---

convention, too, would lead to difficulties, especially when Levinas, after having analyzed the opposition between the Same and the Other in an abstract sense, states the thesis that the Other (*l'Autre*) is *Autrui*. Here *Autrui* cannot be translated by 'the Other' because 'the Other is the Other' would miss the point completely. In this and similar sentences we have therefore translated *Autrui* by 'the human Other' (or 'the human other')."

33. Levinas, *Totality and Infinity*, 72.
34. Ibid.
35. Ibid., 101.
36. Levinas, "Freedom and Command," in Lingis, *Collected Philosophical Papers*, 19.
37. Ibid.
38. Waldenfels, "Levinas and the Face of the Other," in Critchley and Bernasconi, *Cambridge Companion to Levinas*, 69–70.
39. Levinas, *Totality and Infinity*, 101.
40. Morgan, *Discovering Levinas*, 72.

points out that the self of others reveals them through such epiphany as the infinite being:

> The relation between the Other and me, which dawns forth in this expression, issues neither in number nor in concept. The Other remains infinitely transcendent, infinitely foreign; his face in which his epiphany is produced and which appeals to me breaks with the world that can be common to us, whose virtualities are inscribed in our *nature* and developed by our existence.[41]

The face brings the first signification to establish its signification itself into being. Levinas says that "the epiphany that is produced as a face is not constituted as are all other beings, precisely because it 'reveals' infinity. Signification is infinity, that is, the Other."[42] Thus, the existence of the other is the signification of infinity, and infinity has signification when the other's face reveals itself in the relation among beings. Namely, the other's face has its absoluteness because the epiphany occurs as a face.[43]

The face, however, does not reveal its epiphany with its formation of glorification or power; rather, it is revealed in the weakness and powerlessness of such as orphans, widows, the bereaved, and the destitute.[44] This is the ethical characteristic of the face. For instance, the face opens the possibility of murder, the total negation, because "the other is the sole being I can wish to kill" when the I exercises, enjoys and acknowledges a power.[45] Levinas argues that the possibility of murder, paradoxically, opens the ethical resistance against the power because the infinity of being is stronger than the power of murder in that "the infinite paralyses power by its infinite resistance to murder in the nudity of the absolute openness of the Transcendent."[46] Levinas demonstrates the epiphany of the face that

> there is here a relation not with a very great resistance, but with some absolutely *other*: the resistance of what has no resistance—the ethical resistance. The epiphany of the face brings forth the possibility of gauging the infinity of the temptation to murder, not only as a temptation to total destruction, but also as the purely

---

41. Levinas, *Totality and Infinity*, 194.
42. Ibid., 207.
43. Ibid., 196.
44. Ibid., 213–15.
45. Ibid., 198.
46. Ibid., 199.

ethical impossibility of this temptation and attempt.... The epiphany of the face is ethical.[47]

Likewise, the comprehension of this ethical aspect of the face, like the destitute and the hungry, is based on expression and discourse with an ethical paradox in the approach of the I to the Other: the expression seems to impose me to restrict my freedom, but it promotes my freedom while the I arouses my goodness through the order of obligation to respond to the Other.[48] Thus, expression as the formation of response is the basic condition of ethics in Levinas.

The Trace of the Face: Proximity

Levinas discusses the phenomenality of the face of the Other in terms of the signification of the face, the matter of discourse, the issue of truth and justice, and the epiphany of the face in his early works, in particular in *Totality and Infinity*, as above. Levinas develops his philosophical thoughts as he keeps inquiring into the trace of the face of the Other in his later works, especially in *Otherwise than Being or Beyond Essence*. Mark C. Taylor cites Lingis in his book *Altarity* in order to demonstrate the trace of the face: "From measurable and from uncharted distances, another's alien existence can concern us, can contest us. What suffers in him can seem to us the cipher of an order that commands us. Yet one can use the other for entertainment, for instruction, for enrichment, for the exercise of one's sovereignty."[49] Taylor asks two questions about the face: "Why is the face always the face of an other and not my own? It is possible to face the face—without defacing it?"[50] Taylor finds these questions out of the interpretation of the trace of the face in Levinas such as the response/responsibility to the face, and the proximity of the face.

For Levinas, the face of the Other is "a trace of itself, given over to my responsibility, but to which I am wanting and faulty."[51] It is coming through the responsibility of the I for the morality and the sense of guilt for the

---

47. Ibid.
48. Ibid., 200.
49. Taylor, *Altarity*, 209. The original citation is from Lingis, *Excesses*, 113.
50. Ibid.
51. Levinas, *Otherwise than Being*, 91.

survival of the Other.[52] Therefore, the phenomenality of the face initiates the trace in that the face has the extreme possibility of exposure to violence or total negation, that is, nudity. Levinas explained the nudity of face as that

> it escapes representation; it is the very collapse of phenomenality. Not because it is too brutal to appear, but because in a sense too week, non-phenomenon because less than a phenomenon. The disclosing of a face is nudity, non-form, abandon of self, ageing, dying, more naked than nudity. It is poverty, skin with wrinkles, which are a trace of itself.[53]

And also, the bare face has no protection:

> A face approached, a contact with a skin—a face weighted down with a skin, and a skin in which, even in obscenity, the altered face breaths—are already absent from themselves, fallen into the past with an unrecuperable lapse. The skin caressed is not the protection of an organism, simply the surface of an entity; it is the divergency between the visible and the invisible, quasi-transparent, thinner than that which would still justify an expression of the invisible by the visible.[54]

The tenderness of the skin occurs in proximity and immediacy simultaneously with both enjoyment and suffering with the Other. The contact with skin is not only the proximity of the face, but also the "signification beyond being."[55] The appearance of the skin is "an obsession with the other" so that the I has to respond immediately to the face. Here is the trace of the face as the "essential beauty of a face."[56] Levinas posits that face is exposed "to the directness of exposure to invisible death, to a mysterious forlornness."[57] Then, Levinas develops his ethical argument of responsibility through the trace of the face, that is, the summon of the Other

> face facing me, in its expression—in its mortality—summons me, demands me, requires me: as if the invisible death faced by the face of the other—pure alterity, separate, somehow, from any whole— were "my business." . . . It is precisely in that recalling of me to my responsibility by the face that summons me, that demands me,

52. Ibid.
53. Ibid., 88.
54. Ibid., 89–90.
55. Ibid., 90.
56. Ibid.
57. Levinas, *Alterity & Transcendence*, 24.

that require me—it is in that calling into question—that the other is my neighbor.[58]

Thus, responsibility, as the trace of the face, is an unconditional summon of the Other in his or her face as it reveals the gravity of my neighbor.

The face of the Other summons me into "unexceptionable responsibility, preceding every consent, every pact, every contract."[59] The face of my neighbor breaks the phenomenality of a face because of the sense of nakedness of face. The face is too weak to trespass. It's "non-phenomenon" or "less than a phenomenon," and also "this is the *way* of the neighbor is a face."[60] It is proximity of the face. In proximity, the I hears of the command of the face of my neighbor in a sense of disturbance and a suppression of distance as well.[61] Proximity, thus, "opens the distance of a diachrony without a common present, where difference is the past that cannot be caught up with an unimaginable future, the non-representable status of the neighbor behind which I am late and obsessed by the neighbor."[62] Moreover, the I can be in relationship with my neighbor in proximity. Proximity is not a state of repose, but it is a restless place where it demands justice and a simple relation. The closer the I is to my neighbor, the more the I becomes a subject. This relation is not reciprocal, but unique in that the I and the Other do not expect something equal to share. Instead, proximity makes this relationship more just and truthful as it formulates fraternity, that is, the signifyingness of proximity.[63] This signifyingness of proximity makes the I acknowledge that there is a third party alongside the neighbor.[64] The thirdness initiates justice and truth because of the signifyingness of "the-one-for-the-other,"[65] as such: "This 'thirdness' is different from that of the third man, it is the third party that interrupts the face to face of a welcome

---

58. Ibid., 24–25.

59. Levinas, *Otherwise than Being*, 88.

60. Ibid.

61. Ibid., 89.

62. Ibid.

63. Levinas uses signifyingness, in order to explain the linguistic feature of the face through his interpretation of the said and saying. Also, he develops the signification of the self, the other, and the foreign in his conception of signifyingness. I will study more about this point later in my third section of this chapter. See also, *Otherwise than Being*, 46–48, 79–85, 181–85.

64. Ibid., 82–83.

65. Ibid., 85.

of the other man, interrupts the proximity or approach of the neighbor, it is the third man with which justice begins."⁶⁶ This thirdness is based on a trace of relationship as "*unrightness* itself" rather than as "the correlation" between signified and the signification. This signifyingness of the transcendence of the face uniquely opens us to "enter into an immanent *order*."⁶⁷ "Beyond being" is the order of a face, and "*Beyond being is a third person*" in that

> it is the possibility of this third direction of radical *unrightness* which escapes the bipolar play of immanence and transcendence proper to being, where immanence always wins against transcendence. Through a trace the irreversible past takes on the profile of a "He." The *beyond* from which a face comes is in the third person. . . . The *illeity* of the third person is the condition for the irreversibility.⁶⁸

The illeity of the third party (*He*) is not the *it* as Buber accounts more the relation of *I and Thou* than the *it*, but the encounter of the I and He is "in the face itself."⁶⁹ Levinas concludes that "a face is of itself visitation and transcendence. But a face, wholly open, can at the same time be in itself because it is in the trace of illeity."⁷⁰

Simultaneously, the image of God can be seen by the proximity of God, as *the* trace, among beings in terms of the notion of the epiphany and the nakedness of the face. Levinas asks the meaning of suffering through the relation between the I and the Other, and discusses the encounter of the face related to proximity, responsibility, and obsession with the other, being-one-for-the-other.⁷¹ This is the question of the *signification* beyond *being*.⁷² This question makes him inquire of the more ultimate or absolute being. Namely, he finds the answer of this question through the epiphany of the face:

> The nakedness of the face is an extirpation from the context of the world, form the world signifying as a context. The face is precisely that through which the exceptional event of the *facing* [*en-face*]

---

66. Ibid., 150.
67. Levinas, "The Trace of the Other," in Taylor, *Deconstruction in Context*, 355.
68. Ibid., 356.
69. Ibid., 359.
70. Ibid.
71. Levinas, *Otherwise than Being*, 90.
72. Ibid.

Part II: Emmanuel Levinas

is produced, which the façade of the building and of things can only imitate. But this relation of the *coram* is also the most naked nakedness, the "defenseless" and "without resources" itself, the destitution and poverty of absence that constitutes the proximity of God—the trace.[73]

Based on this notion of the trace, Levinas articulates the trace of Infinity, or the Word of God. He says, "A God that concerns me by a Word [*parole*] expressed in the guise of the face of the other is a transcendence that never becomes immanence. The face of the other is his way of signifying."[74] The trace is the way to recognize the voice of God in the face because God speaks for "the first time" through the encounter with the Other.[75] Levinas exemplifies the parable of Jesus concerning the final judgment in Matthew 25, as the trace of God in proximity as such:[76] "The relation to God is presented there as a relation to another person. It is not a metaphor: in the other, there is a real presence of God. In my relation to the other, I hear the Word of God. . . . I'm not saying that the other is God, but that in his or her Face I hear the Word of God."[77] This relation to God, as the relation to the Other, has also an ethical implication as the trace to God is ethics rather than the religious life, especially the liturgy in our life as:

> I would lie to fix it with the term "liturgy." We must for the moment remove from this term every religious signification, even if a certain idea of God should become visible, as a trace, at the end of our analysis. Liturgy, as an absolutely patient action, does

---

73. Levinas, "A Man-God?," in *Entre Nous*, 57.
74. Levinas, *Alterity & Transcendence*, 169.
75. Ibid., 175.
76. John Llewelyn demonstrates Levinas's religious thoughts related to ethics in his book *Emmanuel Levinas*, as he cited Matthew 25 in his chapter "Atheology," 149–61. Llewelyn argues that Levinas's features of the trace of God gives us an answer against the claim of the death of God of Nietzsche. Llewelyn writes in p. 160, "Another, though inevitably still not unenigmatic clue to the way an entry into the Book may be an entry into a humanism that is neither specifically Jewish nor specifically Christian is provided by Levinas's citation of the New Testament in support of his claim that although the Other is not to be identified with God, the Word of God is heard in the Other's face (*visage*), that is to say in his or her looking to me. According to Matthew 25, when those on the Lord's right hand and on his left protest that they have neither given nor refused food, drink or shelter to Him, they are told 'Inasmuch as ye have don't it unto one of the least of my brethren ye have done it unto me.'"
77. Levinas, "Philosophy, Justice, and Love," interview with Levinas, in *Entre Nous*, 110.

not take its place as a cult alongside of works and of ethics. It is ethics itself.[78]

The trace is ethics, not because it obliges us to obey the religious laws or rules, but because it makes us listen to the Word of God and respond to the trace of God in the proximity of the face of the Other.

Hence, for Levinas, the face of the Other is the driving force of his philosophy and ethics. Levinas doubts the manifestation of European ontology as one of the main sources of totalitarianism as he experienced the Second World War and the Holocaust. Instead, Levinas accounts the face of the Other as responsible as he sees the phenomenality of the face, infinity, and the trace of the face, proximity. The face is the epiphany to oblige us to respond immediately. Ethics is initiated by this *response-ability* in that the trace of the face in proximity causes us to hear of the summon of our neighbor, the third party, and the Word of God.[79] Thus, ethics becomes the "first philosophy" rather than ontology.[80] Based on these features of

---

78. Levinas, "Trace of the Other," in Taylor, *Deconstruction in Context*, 349–50.

79. I use this etymological approach of *response-ability* in order to catch the sense of responsibility in Levinas. This *response-ability* does not come from the individual capability that a person, as an autonomous self, is capable to respond to the Other. Instead, this *response-ability* is originated by my recognition that the only thing that the I *is able to* do is to respond to the Infinity of the Other, the summon of the face of my neighbor. The I is obliged to respond to this unconditional summon. This is the unique way of my communication with the other. And this is the basis of Levinas's ethics as "first philosophy."

Levinas says, "To be obliged to respond is no small thing. It is not necessary to approach it in its derivative and banal stage. It is not the formality of some judicial interrogation leaning on public strength. There is here an extraordinary obedience—service without servitude!—to the uprightness of the face of the other man whose irrecusable imperative does not proceed from a threat and whose incomparable authority commands across a suffering precisely as the word of God. It is there that God probably comes to mind. Response demanded in the obligation, though never exhaustive and never annulling responsibility. I would like to step back from the very language of communication to this response demanded, just as I would like to return the psychism of consciousness back to the theo-logy of the idea of infinity" (*Is It Righteous to Be*, 283).

I will discuss this aspect of *response-ability* throughout this book, especially in section 3, part B. Both words of responsibility and response-ability have the same implication of the significance of the response to the Other. I usually use both words with the same implication. When I cite this word from other sources, I will follow the same usage. I will use the word "response-ability" when I need to express of the unique traits of responsibility, especially in section 3, part B.

80. I have an interesting observation in terms of the study of ethics and ontology as I observe the different thoughts on ethics between Emmanuel Levinas and Paul Tillich. Both philosophers began their philosophical struggles through their experiences of the possibility of the total negation of beings during the Second World War. Levinas

Part II: Emmanuel Levinas

the face, I will discuss the issue of intersubjectivity with several important philosophical concepts of Levinas in the next chapter.

---

was delving into the manifestation of the face of the other and responsibility and he argued ethics as first philosophy instead of ontology, as I discussed above; whereas, Tillich placed more emphasis on ontology as his ethical foundation. Tillich argued that the courage to be, to be a part, is the main source of ethics. Thus, the participation of being in beings is the ethical way to be against the power of nonbeing. For further discussion, see Tillich, *Love Power, and Justice, Courage to Be,* and *Morality and Beyond*.

Chapter 3

The Same and the Other

BESIDES THE PHENOMENOLOGICAL INTERPRETATION of the face of the Other, the idea of intersubjectivity and inter-human is another main philosophical theme in Levinas. The analysis of intersubjectivity is initiated by the question of ontology which counts on the autonomous self. Levinas asks the significance of the autonomous self. Then, he attempts to figure out the limitation of Western ontology and to propose a different foundation for human relation, intersubjectivity or inter-human. Besides this question of ontology, I will discuss the human condition as I delve into Levinas's account of alterity related to one of his main philosophical terms, "substitution," in this chapter.

Autonomy or Heteronomy?

According to Levinas, the claim of truth in Western philosophy is based on the idea of freedom and identity (or the Same), that is, the basis of Western philosophy is egology.[1] He argues that autonomy is innate in this assurance of freedom and identity which seems clearly to separate autonomy from

---

1. Levinas, "Philosophy and the Idea of Infinity," in Lingis, *Collective Philosophical Papers*, 47–50, and *Totality and Infinity*, 42–48. Levinas argues the main philosophical features of Western philosophers, especially Kant, Hegel, Husserl, and Heidegger, in order to develop his criticism of egology. See "Phenomenology," in Davis, *Levinas*, to understand Hegel, Husserl, and Heidegger. Also see Paul Davies, "Sincerity and the End of Theodicy," in Critchley and Bernasconi, *Cambridge Companion to Levinas*, in terms of a study of Kant. Also, Peperzak's commentary of Levinas's article "Philosophy and the Idea of Infinity" gives us several good explanations of Levinas's thought of egology. See Peperzak, *To the Other*, 38–72.

39

heteronomy. Autonomy, based on idea of the freedom, has reduced *the other* to *the same*, which creates a formula: "the conquest of being by man over the course of history." This reduction is man's ego.[2] Levinas doubts this phenomenon of egology in Western philosophy: "The structure of the free will becoming *goodness* is not like the glorious and self-sufficient spontaneity of the I and of happiness, which would be the ultimate movement of being; it is, as it were, its converse."[3] Thus, the life of freedom finds itself as it is unjust. Paradoxically, "the life of freedom *in heteronomy*" leads us to the sense of the infinite shift of freedom, that is, an exigency for the I toward my *response-ability*. That is the Infinity of the face, prior to my freedom.[4] Here is a provocative question: "Does there exist a signifyingness of signification which would not be equivalent to the transmutation of the other into the same? Can there be something as strange as an experience of the absolutely exterior, as contradictory in its terms as a heteronomous experience?"[5]

Levinas explores the manifestation of subjectivity and human relation as it is not autonomous, but heteronomous, as he understands the *response-ability* of the I to the face of the Other, the Infinity, in terms of the sense of obedience to the Other in order to answer these questions. For Levinas, transcendence is in immanence, which is "the strange structure (or the *depth*) of the psyche as a soul within the soul."[6] This structure brings the *Same* back into the *Other* because of the "most intimate identity to the *Other*." This is an ultimacy of the Other in that the I (the Same) cannot isolate the self from the Other because of the infinite relationship. The more the I rationally wants to be separated, the more the I sees the ultimacy of this structure.[7] Levinas demonstrates this structure as it shows us the freedom of heteronomy:

> Here the Other [*Autre*], instead of alienating the uniqueness of the Same that he troubles and holds, only calls the Same from the depths of himself toward what is deeper than himself; there where nothing and no one can replace him. Would this already be toward

---

2. Levinas, "Philosophy and the Idea of Infinity," 48 (italics by Levinas).
3. Ibid., 58.
4. Ibid., 58–59 (italics mine).
5. Levinas, "The Trace of the Other," 348.
6. Levinas, "From Consciousness to Wakefulness," in *Of God Who Comes to Mind*, 24.
7. Ibid.

The Same and the Other

responsibility for the other [*autrui*]? The Other calling the Same at and to the depths of himself! This is heteronomy of freedom that the Greeks have not taught us. Transcendence in immanence—this is precisely the nonbelonging of the I to the tissues of its states of consciousness, which thus in their immanence do not stiffen by themselves.[8]

Likewise, this relationship is reflective rather than intentional since it is so urgent that the I does not have any critical knowledge of the self and the Other without the recognition of human relation. This relation is conditional because it is reflective in "its movement against nature."[9] Thus,

> Pure reflection cannot have the first word: how could it arise in the dogmatic spontaneity of a force which moves by itself? Reflection must be put into question from without. Reflection needs a certain kind of heteronomy. Nonetheless, pure reflection cannot have the last word, for it remains essentially naïve insofar as it is an act addressed to a theme. The most radical critique cannot be achieved in a secondary intention which would be immune from critique like a new act of naïveté.[10]

This reflective self-critique comes after responsibility to the infinite, not because the self is staying with the naïve notion of "the more I am just, the more I am guilty," but because the self becomes more reflective into his or her *response-ability* to the command of the infinite.[11] The self holds to his or her subjectivity as responsible as the self listens to the command of the Other. Therefore, heteronomy is stronger than autonomy, not because heteronomy makes subjectivity be a slave of bondage, but because it promotes the purer and more formal relationship between the I and the Other.[12]

In order to comprehend the commandment, based on responsibility, Levinas argues that it is a prerequisite for us to obey the commandment of the summon of the face. The commandment is not justifying any force from outside, nor proceeding from any force, but it comes from the control of one's power through the way of the face of the Other, "as renouncing its force and whatever is all-powerful."[13] The commandment is not only "the

---

8. Ibid.
9. Levinas, "Transcendence and Height," in *Basic Philosophical Writings*, 21.
10. Ibid.
11. Ibid. (italics mine).
12. Levinas, "Philosophy, Justice, and Love," 111.
13. Levinas, *Time and the Other*, 113.

heteronomy of an irrecusable authority," but it also is "the whole novelty of ethics" because the disobedience cannot refute the authority or the goodness of this commandment.[14] The true heteronomy does not come from our superficial obedience to our consciousness or inclination, but it comes from the love for the master with the servile soul which is not capable of being ordered. Again, it is not the sense of slavery or bondage, but it is the love and the fear toward the master, that the fear "fills the soul to such an extent that one no longer sees it, but sees from its perspective."[15] The servile soul, created by this obedience, is "the most painful experience of modern man," because he or she has to refute the freedom of humanity:

> Human freedom is essentially unheroic. That one could, by intimidation, by torture, break the absolute resistance of freedom, even in its freedom of thought, that an alien order no longer hits us in the face, that we could accept it as though it came from ourselves, show how derisible is our freedom.[16]

Thus, the commandment of the face does not guarantee the freedom of the self any longer as autonomous as it is; rather, it inspires us to be a servile soul as the heteronomous self who loves the master in spite of the most painful experience of refutation of freedom.[17] Finally, this servile soul leads us to obey the transcendence, which is called Divinity or God, in that the absoluteness of obedience makes us recognize the absolute order, the word of God, which is revealed by the epiphany of the face of the Other.[18] This absolute order, the word of God, brings us to the realm of the eventuality of Infinity which is beyond our autonomous features such as our memories,

---

14. Ibid.
15. Levinas, "Freedom and Command," in *Collective Philosophical Papers*, 16.
16. Ibid.
17. Ibid.
I would like to introduce a poem, titled "Obedience," written by Yong Woon Hahn, a Buddhist monk, and social activist against the Japanese Colonization period in Korea. I think that this poem allows for a creative conversation with the notion of obedience for Levinas. I translated this myself.
"Obedience"
People say that they love freedom; yet, I love obedience.
Of course, I know freedom well, but I would love to give only obedience to you.
It is even sweeter than the beauty of freedom that I obey the one whom I want to obey. That is my happiness.
You command me to obey other people, yet, only that commandment, I cannot obey.
Because, if I were to obey others, I could not obey you.
18. Levinas, *Alterity & Transcendence*, 35.

Inter-human and Asymmetry

The question of being is not the matter of the ontology of humanity, but it is the matter of the inter-human which comes from the absoluteness of the Other, especially from the epiphany of the face. Again, the question of being does not count for the understanding of being, *per se*, in that "the understanding of a being consists in going beyond that being—precisely into openness—and perceiving it upon the *horizon of being*."[20] Based on this comprehension of the human being, Levinas asks, "how can the *relation with being* be, from the outset, anything other than its *comprehension* as being, the fact of freely letting it be inasmuch as it is being?"[21] Levinas's answer is not in the manifestation of the self, but in the Transcendence or the Infinity of the Other, that is called as "religion" by Levinas.[22] In terms of the comprehension of the self and transcendence, Calvin Schrag demonstrates that transcendence plays the dialectic between the self and community as self-constitutional, as the self encounters the other.[23] Thus, transcendence is

---

19. Levinas, *Time and the Other*, 114.

I think that Paul Tillich could have a good conversation with Levinas in terms of the concept of the ethics of heteronomy. Tillich develops his ethical thought based on the concept of *agape*, the unconditional love of God and theonomy. He analyzes the independent reaction of autonomy for humanity toward heteronomy as he explains historical backgrounds of the church and the secular. He argues that the heteronomous tradition of the church seemed to be theonomous, but it was not true in that it was intentional without any sense of the autonomy of humanity. Thus, he esteems more autonomous values in ethics than heteronomous values as he says, "Intentional theonomy is heteronomy and must be rejected by ethical research. Actual theonomy is autonomous ethics under the Spiritual Presence" (*Systematic Theology*, 3:268). I believe that Tillich and Levinas approached ethics in a different conceptual process of heteronomy and autonomy, but, on the other hand, there are a few comparative points like participation and responsibility between Tillich's theonomy and Levinas's obedience and heteronomy. In order to have further discussion, see *Systematic Theology*, vol. 3, part 3, 162–282, and *Theology of Culture*, ch. 10, 133–45.

20. Levinas, "Is Ontology Fundamental?," 5.
21. Ibid.
22. Ibid., 8.
23. Schrag, *Self after Postmodernity*, 111.

operant not only in the face-to-face encounter with the other self as other, but also in the self's recognition that the totality of received social practices exceeds its particular hold on the world. The holistic matrix and referential interdependence of social practices and communal involvements transcend the particular discourses and actions of embodied agents.[24]

At this point, the issue of transcendence is not the matter of the dynamics of "transcendence-within-immanence," which is related to the notion of "the economies of the human subject" in their actions, perceptions, or involvements with the world; rather, transcendence is the "radical exteriority," in the philosophical idea of infinity in Levinas.[25] Schrag analyzes the threefold function of transcendence: "as a principle of protest against cultural hegemony," "as a condition for a transversal unification that effects a convergence without coincidence," and "as a power of giving without expectation of return."[26] Therefore, transcendence works as "a robust alterity" as such: "Responding to the beckoning of this otherness of transcendence, the wayfaring self struggles for a self-understanding and a self-constitution within the constraints of an irremovable finitude."[27]

With this sense alterity and transcendence, Levinas interprets the human condition of suffering based on this inter-human perspective. Suffering cannot be comprehended properly with the consciousness of the common destiny of human being. It has to be perceived by the inter-human perspective that "lies in a non-indifference of one to another," and "in a responsibility of one for another."[28] Edward Farley analyzes human reality as the being as inter-human, as he follows Levinas's perspective of inter-human as follows:

> *The interhuman is primary to both agents and the social because it is the sphere that engenders the criterion, the face, for the workings of the other spheres. . . . Individual agents are irreducible, complex, and multi-dimentional. . . . The human from of life, like all living things, actively strives, effortfully acts, and responds. . . . The spheres of agency, the interhuman, and the social are mixes of causalities*

---

24. Ibid.
25. Ibid., 114.
26. Ibid., 148.
27. Ibid.
28. Levinas, "Useless Suffering," in *Entre Nous*, 100.

*(influences), perduring structure and transcending. . . . The most general feature of our human condition is its tragic character.*²⁹

Farley accounts Levinas's understanding of alterity and intersubjectivity *of and among* people in order to "explore human vulnerability, human desire, and social being, and how these things function when transformed by both evil and redemption."³⁰ Farley recapitulates:

> The face is also a summons to felt obligation. That which distinguishes compassion from pity, namely being drawn toward the other's fragility, is also what gives the summons the characters of felt obligation. When we are summoned by the face, we are alerted to the objective predicament of the other. This would be the attitude of charity in the cold-blooded sense of a self-serving act. Being summoned by the fragility of the other not only evokes a suffering-with (compassion) but also suffering-for (obligation). Obligation is a posture or disposition that comes into being as a hearing and felt response to the summons of the face.³¹

Likewise, the conceptualization of "suffering-with" and "suffering-for" in Farley is relevant to the account of responsibility and obedience in this the inter-human perspective. Responsibility does not rely on the reciprocal human relationship since my *response-ability* is prior to the moment of reciprocity.³² The reciprocity between the I and the Other is not sufficient for us to get the sense of responsibility because it is contractual. In this contractual relationship, the I falls into "natural egotism" even if it guarantees the social and political orders for and among citizens. Instead, through the analyses of "useless suffering," Levinas insists that the resource of human relation is "in the inter-human perspective of *my* responsibility for the other, without concern for reciprocity, in my call for his or her disinterested help, in the asymmetry of the relation of *one* to the *other*."³³

Hence, inter-human relation does not rely on the symmetrical reciprocity any longer, but it is founded on the asymmetrical relatedness of the humanities. One of the philosophical foundations of Levinas is Russian writers like Pushkin, Tolstoy, Lermontov, Turgenev, Gogol, and Dostoevsky.³⁴

---

29. Farley, *Good and Evil*, 28–29 (italics original).
30. Ibid., 33 (italics mine).
31. Ibid., 42–43.
32. Levinas, "Useless Suffering," 100–101 (italics mine).
33. Ibid., 101.
34. Levinas, *Ethics and Infinity*, 22.

Part II: Emmanuel Levinas

In particular, Dostoevsky gave critical ideas to Levinas: "metaphysical desire for the other and the asymmetrical relation of responsibility."[35] Levinas criticizes Martin Buber's understanding of human relationship of *I and Thou* as it is based on reciprocity, and then, Levinas accounts for Dostoevsky, as Levinas cites two essential phrases from *The Brothers Karamazov*: "We are all responsible for everyone else—but I am more responsible than all the others," and "Each of us is guilty before everyone and for everything, and I more than the others."[36] The expression of "more than all the others" is an axiomatic initiative of asymmetrical human relationship in Levinas. He argues:

> He does not mean that every "I" is more responsible than all the others, for that would be to generalize the law for everyone else—to demand as much from the other as I do from myself. The essential asymmetry is the very basis of ethics: not only am I more responsible than the other but I am even responsible for everyone else's responsibility![37]

The responsibility of the I is not transferable, nor interchangeable in that nobody can replace the I. Only this responsible I can grasp the concept of the responsibility for the Other.[38] Now, the I and the Other formulate their relationship as inter-human, which does not come from reciprocity, but is initiated by asymmetry. Inter-human is not in an intentional self-consciousness of human relationship; rather, it is in a hostage situation of the I for the Other, that is "substitution."[39] The saying of "here I am" means that the I becomes a witness to the Infinity of the Other. The subjectivity of the I is not prior to the Other's face, but it calls himself or herself in front of the Other as a witness to the Infinite.[40] "Here I am," therefore, "I can substitute myself for everyone, but no one can substitute himself for me."[41]

---

35. Willian Edelglass, "Asymmetry and Normativity: Levinas Reading Dostoevsky on Desire, Responsibility, and Suffering," in Tymieniecka, *Enigma of Good and Evil*, 712.

36. Levinas, *Is It Righteous to Be?*, 72, 135; *Face to Face with Levinas*, 31; *Ethics and Infinity*, 98, 101; and *Otherwise than Being*, 146.

37. Levinas, *Face to Face with Levinas*, 31.

38. Levinas, *Ethics and Infinity*, 100–101.

39. Ibid., 100. Levinas, *Otherwise than Being*, 146.

40. Levinas, *Otherwise than Being*, 146.

41. Levinas, *Ethics and Infinity*, 101.

The Same and the Other
An-archy and Substitution

Levinas quotes Paul Célan in German, "Ich bin du, wenn ich ich bin" (I am you, if [or whenever] I am I), as Levinas develops his thoughts of subjectivity and transcendence related to "substitution," that is, an-archial experience in human relation.[42] Again, Levinas criticizes that the Western notion of subjectivity as consciousness comes from the knowledge of the "thematic exposition of Being," which is initiated by "the rediscovery of being on the basis of an ideal principle or *arche* (ἀρχή) in its thematic exposition."[43] The proximity of the Other in human relationship, however, tells us that subjectivity is not based on the *arche* of consciousness because "proximity is always 'already past,' above the 'now' which it troubles and obsesses."[44] Levinas's terminology, "anarchy," thus, does not mean the chaotic disorder in the human condition, but it means the pre-original condition of human being.[45] Taylor explains that "anarchy 'is' a radical ante that is 'incommensurable with every present.' . . . Levinas's *anarchie* is a past 'more ancient than every representable origin, a pre-original and anarchial *passed*.' Instead of an absolute origin (*arche*), the *an-archie* renders impossible every origin and all originality. Everything, everybody is ever after, i.e., never primary, always secondary."[46] The an-archial, pre-original condition, related to the proximity of the Other, makes the I value my *response-ability* to the Other, that is, this responsibility "*is justified by no prior commitment.*" No "me-ontological" and "metalogical" structure, nor the consciousness of "self-control and commands." Responsibility of the I is absolute because it does not count any "a priori," nor the thematization of human being.[47] The an-archial human condition shows us the unique interpretation of the relation between the I and the Other of Levinas with the German phrase, "*Ich bin du, wenn ich ich bin*" (I am you if [whenever] I am I).

This subjectivity is "the one-for-the-other subjectivity," which does not originate by any sense of "the generosity of a voluntary act," related to the reciprocal relationship, but it is initiated by the "extradition to the

---

42. Levinas, *Otherwise than Being*, 99.

43. Levinas, "Substitution," in *Basic Philosophical Writings*, 80. I added the Greek word of *arche*. The Greek word, ἀρχή, means origin or principle.

44. Ibid., 81.

45. Ibid.

46. Taylor, "Infinity—Emmanuel Levinas," 193. The direct citation of this article comes from *Otherwise than Being*, 9.

47. Levinas, *Otherwise than Being*, 100–102.

other."[48] This extradition to the other is the foundation of *response-ability* in Levinas. The responsibility for the other, therefore, is not only "an-archy," pre-original, since it is not the quantity of the beginning to the end of freedom in terms of a voluntary decision, but it also is the testimony of the infinity which is glorious and saintly.[49] Levinas recapitulates:

> Responsibility for the other precedes every decision, it is before the origin, An-archy. Here, the without-beginning is nevertheless not the bad infinity of the extrapolation of the present by pure negation, since responsibility moves positively toward the other.... My responsibility for the other is precisely this relation with an unthematizable Infinity. It is neither the experience of Infinity nor proof of it: it *testifies* to Infinity.[50]

This testimony does not belong to a "subjective experience" of the proclamation of the "ontological 'conjuncture' disclosed to the subject," but it does to "the very glory of the Infinite."[51] The glory of the Infinite is the response to the summons of the face of the Other as the I develops "sincerity or Saying." Sincerity is the Saying itself in that sincerity is completed by the Saying without any senses of control in the human being.[52] Saying as "the pure transparency of a confession" is this testimony.[53] The Saying

---

48. Levinas, "Truth of Disclosure and Truth of Testimony," in *Basic Philosophical Writings*, 102–3.

49. Ibid., 103.

50. Ibid.

51. Ibid.

52. Levinas develops his philosophical thoughts of language with his terminology of "Saying" and "the Said," mainly in his book *Otherwise than Being*. Simon Critchley explains these features briefly in the introduction of the *Cambridge Companion to Levinas* (17–18), such that "the saying is ethical and the said is ontological. Although Levinas can hardly be said to offer dictionary definitions of these terms, we might say that the saying is my exposure—both corporeal and sensible—to the other person, my inability to resist the other's approach. It is the performative stating, proposing or expressive position of myself facing the other. It is a verbal and possibly also non-verbal ethical performance, of which the essence cannot be captured in constative propositions. It is, of you will, a performative *doing* that cannot be reduced to a propositional description. By contrast, the said is a statement, assertion or proposition of which the truth or falsity can be ascertained. To put it another way, one might say that the content of my words, their identifiable meaning, is the said, while the saying consists in the fact that these words are being addressed to an interlocutor, at this moment each of you. The saying is nonthematizable ethical residue of language that escapes comprehension, interrupts ontology and is the very enactment of the movement from the same to the other."

53. Ibid.

The Same and the Other

as testimony paves the way before all sayings as the I exposes himself or herself to the summon of the face of the Other, the glory of the Infinite. The glory of the Infinite "commands me from my own mouth." The commandment from my own mouth has a very exceptional and unique "structure" in which the testimony disappears in front of this glory of the Infinite.[54] This is an anarchic reversal of heteronomy into autonomy, in that the way of the Infinite comes to pass all metaphors of the laws in self-consciousness, and even the metaphors of reconciliation between autonomy and heteronomy. This is an enigma of the "an-archic response" in the responsibility of the I to the Other. This is the enigmatic conception of an-archy in Levinas's ethical initiative of responsibility.[55]

Based on this proposal of the condition of an-archy in human relation, Levinas articulates his thought of Infinity with the illustration of the relation between selfhood (ipseity) and otherness (alterity). Along with the general philosophical thought of existence, Levinas inquires about the disclosure of being, and he poses the issue of "*essence* as a perpetual vigilance and self-possession."[56] He argues that "the disclosure of being to itself involves a *recurrence*," and the issue of recurrence has its own issue of "the Same," "the knot of ipseity," and "the play of *consciousness*."[57] He asks several questions about these issues: "What is the relation between the 'oneself' and the *for self* of representation?" "Is the 'oneself' a recurrence of the same type as consciousness, knowledge, and representation, all of which would be sublimated in consciousness conceived as Mind?" And, "Is the 'oneself' consciousness in its turn, or is it not a quite distinct event, one which would justify the use of separate terms: Self, I, Ego, soul?"[58] Then, he explains "the identity of ipseity" in order to find an answer about these questions:

> To be sure, reflection *upon* the self is possible, but this reflection does not *constitute* the living *recurrence* of subjectivity, a recurrence without duality, but a unity without rest, whose un-rest is due neither to dispersion of exterior givens nor to the flux of time biting into the future while conserving a past. The living identity

---

54. Ibid., 103–4.
55. Ibid., 105. See also Levinas, "Enigma and Phenomenon," in *Basic Philosophical Writing*, 65–77.
56. Levinas, "Substitution," in *Basic Philosophical Writings*, 83. Levinas published this article in 1967, and he also modified this article in chapter 4 of *Otherwise than Being* (1974). This chapter has almost similar contents to the former article.
57. Levinas, "Substitution," 83.
58. Ibid.

of oneself is not distinguished from the self and does not lend itself to either a synthetic activity or recollection or anticipation. To present the knot of ipseity which is tied into the straight thread of *essence* according to the model of intentionality of the *for itself*, or as an opening on the self, is to presuppose a new ipseity behind ipseity. Ipseity is an indefeasible unity that has never been separated from the self.[59]

This restlessness of ipseity cannot make being enter into "discourse, to be thematized, and to appear to consciousness";[60] rather, it experiences the un-rest "ontological adventures" such as negativity of nonbeing, recurrence of contraction of being, and persecution of "the an-archic passivity of obsession."[61] These negativities, contraction, and passivity are the ontological categories that make ipseity become "a hostage" of the Other. Levenas says, "The word 'I' means to be answerable for everything and for everyone."[62]

This is the moment to ask the meaning of the Infinite and the Transcendent. This is the place from whence our responsibility comes. This is the future of being which goes through the ontological adventure of ipseity. Now, ipseity encounters alterity as the self experiences of the Infinite and the Transcendent. Levinas recapitulates, "This way of being, without prior commitment, responsible for the other, amounts to the fact of human fellowship, prior to freedom."[63] With this process of fellowship, the human being experiences the absoluteness of alterity, related to the Infinity and the Transcendence. Levinas elaborates:

> Being takes on a meaning and becomes a universe not because there exists among thinking beings a being pursuing ends, a being thereby structured as an Ego. There is abandonment, obsession, responsibility, and a Self because the trace of the Infinite (exceeding the present, turning its arche into anarchy) is inscribed in proximity. The noninterchangeable par excellence, the I, substitutes itself for others. Nothing is a game. Thus being is transcended.[64]

Thus, it is unconditional that being has to respond to alterity, not because he or she intends to become responsible, but because they are the hostages

59. Ibid., 84.
60. Ibid.
61. Ibid., 85–87.
62. Ibid., 90.
63. Ibld., 91.
64. Ibid.

The Same and the Other

of this ontological absoluteness. This is the moment that the self becomes "to be responsible before having done anything" and "to substitute oneself for others." Substitution is not the proclamation of the universality of "the essence of an Ego," but it is the restoration of the soul in its egoity whence the way of essentialization of the ego "passes through the third party" without any support of generalization.[65] Levinas demonstrates that

> Modern antihumanism, which denies the primacy that the human person, a free end in itself, has for the signification of being, is true over and above the reasons it gives itself. It makes a place for subjectivity positing itself in abnegation, in sacrifice, and in substitution. Its great intuition is to have abandoned the idea of person as an end in itself. The Other is the end, and me, I am hostage.[66]

This hostage condition makes the I have "the unlimited and initial responsibility" that justifies the concern of justice, the self, and philosophy. This is also the moment of "the impossibility of escaping God," that is, "an absolute passivity." Levinas demonstrates this point as such: "This passivity is not simply the possibility of death within being, the possibility of impossibility, but is an impossibility anterior to this possibility, an impossibility of slipping away, an absolute susceptibility, a gravity without any frivolity, the birth of a meaning in the obtuseness of being, a 'being able to die,' submitted to sacrifice."[67] Thus, substitution, to be hostage, is fundamental in human relation, not because it represents to us the servitude of the I to the Other, but because it shows us the way for the restoration of the essence of the ego through responsibility.[68]

For Levinas, thus, human relation between the self and the Other is not based on the concept of the autonomous self any more, but it is relying on the conception of the heteronomous self. Because the commandment of the face of the Other is unconditional and absolute, the self has to respond to the Other, that is, Obedience. This sense of obedience proposes a new comprehension of human relationship, asymmetry. In this asymmetry, the self responds to the Other as "here I am," as "I am your hostage." The hostage condition is substitution in human relation which accounts for the Other more than the I, not because of the self-consciousness of the Other, but because of the sense of absoluteness of alterity which summons me to

---

65. Ibid., 94.
66. Ibid.
67. Ibid., 95.
68. Ibid., 94.

response. Substitution is the source of ethics, that is, the ethics of obedience and the ethics of otherness.

Chapter 4

Ethics, Responsibility and the Human Reality

THE ETHICAL CONSEQUENCES OF Levinas are based on his phenomenological interpretation of the face of the Other, as I discussed above. I will explore here some more details about the ethical thought of Levinas. I will discuss deeply the reason why Levinas accounts for ethics instead of ontology will be discussed. I will explore how and why Levinas develops his ethical foundation in terms of *response-ability*. Then, I will examine Levinas's ethical interpretation of the human reality, and the issues of equality, resistance, justice and peace in this chapter.

Why Ethics?

Robert Gibbs proposes the question of "why" instead of the questions of "what," "how" and "who" in order to articulate his thought of the ethics of responsibility. According to Gibbs, "why" is a basic ethical question because "the question why? opens up a realm of ethics: an ethics of responsibility, of an ability to respond arising in the exigency to attend to another's questioning." Then he asks, "What if a philosopher were, first of all, one who feels the weight of another person's question? What if a philosopher thinks not to be free of all others nor only to befuddle them, but thinks in order to respond to questions that others ask?"[1] Steven Kepnes tries to find an answer to this question of why as such:

1. Gibbs, *Why Ethics?*, 3. Gibbs develops his arguments of ethical responsibility based on the texts and the thoughts of Levinas, Derrida, Rosenzweig, Habermas, Benjamin, the

Part II: Emmanuel Levinas

> Why ethics? Why? Because your beginning is, precisely, not you. Your beginning is in the collective "We." We have given birth to you and We have given you the gift of words and signs and truth. It is your responsibility then, to give back and, actually, to give forward. You have been given and therefore you are responsible to give the gift of life and words and signs to the future.[2]

Likewise, the question of why is also a fundamental inquiry in Levinas in terms of the significance of inter-human relation, the meaning of the Other, the notion of We-ness, the issue of truth, and the importance of ethics for humanity.

Again, Levinas begins his philosophical and ethical thoughts along with his criticism of Western philosophy as its focus on the existence of the individual self is based on symmetrical relationship. Levinas severely criticizes that this symmetry is the main cause of the totalitarianism because this relationship only emphasizes subjectivity and the self, not the outside of self. Instead, Levinas proposes the asymmetrical human relation in order to formulate a new relationship based on the phenomenological existence of others.[3] This argument makes him concentrating on in ethics as he posits that ethics has its unique place as "first philosophy."[4] Levinas brings the terminology "first philosophy" from traditional thoughts on ontology of the twentieth century's Western philosophy, in particular from the tradition of existentialism. He argues that the traditional ontology, which concentrates on individual subjectivity, does not have to be considered as "first philosophy" any longer.[5] Rather, the idea of intersubjectivity needs to be considered as "first philosophy." Levinas's understanding of existence, thus, is not ontological, but ethical, in that ethics is founded on human relation and the significance of alterity. Because ethics, as first philosophy, signifies not only the existence of the self, but also the manifestation of the other, the relationship between self and others, consequently, becomes the main philosophical topic, that is, ethics.

Most of all, the sense of responsibility is the basis of ethics. The dynamics between ipseity and alterity make people responsible for one

---

Bible, the Talmud, Maimonides, and others with his own commentary of these works.

2. Kepnes, "Ethics after Levinas," 115.

3. Levinas, *Totality and Infinity*, 215–16.

4. Peperzak, preface to *Basic Philosophical Writings*, xii; Levinas "Transcendence and Height," 20; and *Totality and Infinity*, 46–47.

5. Levinas, *Totality and Infinity*, 46.

another while they have interactions. This is the pace of response-ability. Again, selfhood, in Levinas, does not come from the inside of a subject, but it comes from this responsibility. He illustrates:

> A disengagement outside (or this side) of being is not the result of an inconsequential game played out in some corner of being where the ontological plot is relaxed. An exit made possible by the weight exerted at a single point by the remainder of its substance: responsibility. It is this responsibility for the creature that constitutes the "self." Responsibility for the creature, for that which the ego had not been the author. To be a "self" is to be responsible before having done anything.[6]

Besides, not only does responsibility make people be "self," but it also lets human beings resist the power of nonbeing.[7] Levinas demonstrates this point with his explanation of the passivity of ipseity:

> Its exceptional unicity in the passibity of the Passion of the Self is the incessant event of substitution, the fact of being emptied of its being, of being turned inside out, the fact of *nonbeing*. . . . It is the ex-ceptional, which cannot serve as the grammatical *category* of Noun or Verb, the recurrence that can only be stated as an *in itself*, or as an *inside-out of being*, or as *nonbeing*. Nonbeing is a matter of bearing the burden of misery and failure of the other, and even the responsibility that the other can have for me. To be a "self" is always to have one degree of responsibility more. The responsibility for the other is perhaps the concrete event designated by the verb "not to be," in an attempt to distinguish it both from nothingness and from the product of the transcendental imagination.[8]

---

6. Levinas, "Substitution," in *Basic Philosophical Writings*, 94.

7. Here is another interesting comparative point related to the resistance against the power of non-being between Levinas and Tillich. Ethics of otherness and responsibility in Levinas is the source to resist the power of total negation of non-being, whereas ontology and the courage to be (participation) in Tillich gives us the sense of the resistance against the power of destruction of beings. Tillich argues that individualization and participation are the ways to struggle against the power of non-being. When the self/selves has/have the notion of self-transcendence, self-integration, and self-creativity, they can formulate religion, morality, and culture as the sources of ontology, the courage to be. Instead of religious oppression, moralism, and monolithic culture, Tillich argues that ontology inspires a new understanding of religion, morality, and ethics. See Tillich, *Courage to Be*, and *Theology of Culture*.

8. Ibid., 91.

Part II: Emmanuel Levinas

When a person acknowledges his or her ipseity and its relation with alterity, they begin to recognize the sense of responsibility, and this recognition of responsibility is the root of resistance against the power of nonbeing. This acknowledgment of responsibility can make people become a "supporter of the universe," from which originates "happiness," because it makes possible "the most radical engagement," that is, "total altruism."[9] Finally, human beings can become ethical, not because of their personal ethical notions, like goals, duty or virtue, but because of their recognition of responsibility into the face of the Other, the Infinity. In other words, Levinas's ethical demand is not based on traditional themes of ethics such as deontology, teleology, areteology, but ethics comes from the acknowledgment of transcendence in intersubjectivity. That is, responsibility is the basic quiddity of ethics in Levinas.

There is a bond between expression and responsibility because the epiphany of infinity is expression and discourse. The ethical condition is formulated by this essence of language in that expression and discourse permit us to extract language from subjection to a preexistent thought. The face opens the primordial discourse that obliges one to enter into discourse.[10] Thus, the discourse creates my obligation to the Other, that is, obedience.[11] Levinas explains the obligation as he states the signification of infinity through the face and consciousness as such: "It is the ethical exigency of the face, which puts into question the consciousness that welcomes it. The consciousness of obligation is no longer a consciousness, since it tears consciousness up from its center, submitting it to the Other."[12] Also, the consciousness of obligation is directly related to the unlimited responsibility to others, the neighbors.[13] The face inspires the ethical responsibility, as the obligation makes me respond to the essential destitution of the Other.[14] Besides, the face commands me to obey the hearing of the other as the form of "original imperative" or "original transcendence."[15] Levinas points out this unconditional status or the uniqueness of responsibility:

---

9. Levinas, "Transcendence and Height," 18.
10. Levinas, *Totality and Infinity*, 200–201.
11. Ibid., 214.
12. Ibid., 207.
13. Levinas, *Alterity & Transcendence*, 30.
14. Levinas, *Totality and Infinity*, 215.
15. Levinas, *Alterity & Transcendence*, 32.

> The face of the neighbor as the bearer of an order, imposing upon me, with respect to the other, a gratuitous and non-transferable responsibility, as if the I were chosen and unique—and in which the other were absolutely other, i.e., still incomparable, and thus unique.[16]

This unlimited responsibility justifies that the face of the neighbor initiates the sense of justice with the philosophical consciousness of the self.

In addition, responsibility redefines that truth is not *Desein*'s respect or comprehension of Being in its disclosedness within-the-world; rather, Manning demonstrates:

> Truth is the face of the Other, the Other's expression of him/herself to me, and appeal made to me and a demand made upon me. Levinas insists that the Other's "appeal to me is his truth." But if truth is appeal, then it does not merely exist, but it has to be produced in that it has to be responded to: "My response is not added as an accident to a 'nucleus' of his objectivity, but first produces his truth." Truth is produced between the subject and the Other when the Other commands the subject in the ethical relation and the subject responds in responsibility.[17]

Manning recapitulates that "ethics, morality and justice are not for Levinas somehow subordinate to truth or an aspect of truth. They are the truth of truth, the highest truth. . . . Thus, the just relation with the Other is not only the essence of ethics, or morality, or justice, but is the essence of truth as well."[18] Thus, truth is "ethics itself," and as such "the highest and most important truth" is ethics, "which Levinas refers to as the *good*."[19] Therefore:

> For Levinas, ethics as first philosophy means that the social relations is that event in being that is not only irreducible to knowledge of being, but is something other than, more than, and better than comprehension of being. Ethics thus overthrows the supremacy of knowledge of being; it puts an end of the "domination of knowledge." Ethics has nothing to do with epistemological power or weakness, but refers to the responsibility that is prior to and the condition of knowing. . . . Thus, it is ethics, which interrupts and

---

16. Ibid., 170.

17. Manning, *Interpreting Otherwise than Heidegger*, 116. The direct citation of Manning of Levinas is from *Totality and Infinity*, 291.

18. Ibid., 117.

19. Ibid. (italics original).

conditions the adventure of knowledge, and not the adventure of knowledge itself, which is first philosophy.[20]

In this sense, the Heideggerian notion of respect for Being, as the process of having truth, does not conceive the manifestation of truth any longer; yet, for Levinas, respect for Being is "truth itself, the highest truth, the Good."[21]

Furthermore, Levinas articulates the issue of justice and the manifestation of truth in his interpretation of the social relation of humanity. Levinas says, "Truth is made possible by relation with the Other, our master. Truth is thus bound up with the social relation, which is justice."[22] The recognition of the Other, my master, is the source of justice. Namely, equality among people is initiated by this recognition of the mastery of the Other.[23] This recognition is the conscience which welcomes the Other as the I questions my power and my freedom as those are, in a sense, to be arbitrary, and in another sense, to be violent. This conscience of welcoming the Other is the commencement of moral consciousness.[24] On the one hand, my freedom is challenged by the Master, and this "sovereign exercise of freedom" makes truth possible.[25] Levinas argues that

> he who speaks to me and across the words proposes himself to me retains the fundamental foreignness of the Other who judges me; our relations are never reversible. The supremacy posits him in himself, outside of my knowing, and it is by relation to this absolute that the *given* takes on meaning.[26]

On the other hand, my freedom to adhere to truth leads me to be conscious of the moral *relation* with the Master. Finally, this moral consciousness teaches me, "the locus of truth is society."[27] Hence, for Levinas, ethics is the "first philosophy," now that ethics is the conceptualization of truth and justice in human relation.

20. Ibid., 118.
21. Ibid., 122.
22. Levinas, *Totality and Infinity*, 72.
23. Ibid.
24. Ibid., 84.
25. Ibid., 101.
26. Ibid.
27. Ibid.

Response-ability

My *response-ability* is initiated by my recognition of an-archy and substitution in the relation between the I and the Other. The Infinite calls the I to say "here I am." That is an-archy, "the impossibility of saying 'no.'"[28] Being responsible is substitution, since the status of hostage of the I to the Other engages us into the situation of obligation "without culpability." My responsibility is "prior to justice that makes distributions, before the measurements of justice," and then, "something terrible" happens to me, that is, "hostage." Thus, "the trace of the infinite is inscribed in my obligation in regard to an other in that moment which corresponds to the call."[29] Levinas articulates the principle of responsibility with the commencement of an-archy. The responsibility does not originate by my commitment or my autonomous moral decision for the Other. Instead:

> The unlimited responsibility in which I find myself comes from the hither side of my freedom, from a "prior to every memory," an "ulterior to every accomplishment," from the non-present par excellence, the non-original, the an-archical, prior to or beyond essence. The responsibility for the other is the locus in which is situated the null-side of subjectivity, where the privilege of the question "Where?" no longer holds. The time of the *said* and of *essence* there lets the pre-original saying be heard, answers to transcendence, to a dia-chrony, to the irreducible divergency that opens here between the non-present and every representable divergency, which in its own way—a way to be clarified—makes a sign to the responsible one.[30]

Likewise, Peperzak describes the feature of responsibility "as a prephenomenal and pre-ontological inspiration." This description of responsibility, however, does not rely on our idea of something ethereal, like the dichotomy of the body and the soul of the traditional anthropology.[31] Rather, Peperzak writes, "Levinas's analyses show that human subjectivity exists as a sensible, affective, working, speaking, and suffering body, whose skin is the possibility of contact, proximity, and vulnerability and whose respiration is the dynamism of a moral inspiration and the expiration of

---

28. Levinas, *Is it Righteous to Be*, 216.
29. Ibid.
30. Levinas, *Otherwise than Being*, 10–11.
31. Peperzak, *Beyond*, 68.

someone who lives for Others who may continue to live after one's death."[32] My *response-ability* to say "here I am" is pre-original, now that it does not show my autonomous capability to be responsible for others as the essence of the subjectivity, but it does how the I follows the summon of the face of the Other, the Infinity.

For Levinas, *response-ability* is the matter of language, as long as the I is obliged to *response* to the Infinity. To respond to the Other is communication, speaking and Saying. According to Peperzak, language in Levinas is "not only and not primarily enunciation, apophansis or expression, but *communication*."[33] This communication formulates human relationship, but this relational aspect of language is forgotten by Western philosophy. Peperzak elaborates communication as the basis of relation as such: "In talking or writing I always address my words—and myself!—to someone: I speak to another person who I suppose hears me. Even if I speak or write to myself, I, the listener or reader of my words, differ from myself as writer or speaker. Speaking or writing, thus, includes necessarily a relation between someone and some Other."[34] Levinas develops the idea of human relationship into his philosophical interpretation of Saying in terms of responsibility. Maintaining this relationship with the Other, the neighbor, is Saying which initiates responsibility in that "saying is to respond to another."[35] That is *response-ability*. This responsibility is unverifiable by me because it is not limited or measured by the memory of the I any longer, but it is "found to be at the mercy of the freedom and the fate of the other man."[36] Here is the paradox of my response-ability, that my response is extremely passive, but this passivity is in "pure saying itself," which is not assumed.[37] Levinas demonstrates that

> the act of saying will turn out to have been introduced here from the start as the supreme passivity of exposure to another, which is responsibility for the free initiatives of the other. Whence there is an "inversion" of intentionality which, for its part, always preserves before deeds accomplished enough "presence of mind" to assume them. There is an abandon of the sovereign and active

32. Ibid.
33. Ibid., 62 (italics original).
34. Ibid.
35. Levinas, *Otherwise than Being*, 47.
36. Ibid.
37. Ibid.

subjectivity, of undeclined self-consciousness, as the subject in the nominative form in an apophansis. And there is in subjectivity's relationship with the other, which we are here striving to describe, a quasi-hagiographic style that wishes to be neither a sermon nor the confession of a "beautiful soul."[38]

Again, responsibility, *per se*, is a passivity "more passive than all passivity in that it is 'exposure of exposedness, expression, and Saying' without any assumption of this exposure or holding back. Responsibility is not only antecedent of my freedom, but it is also the present and representation in this notion of passivity.[39] Responsibility for my neighbor is "the frankness, sincerity, veracity of Saying," in that Saying does not try to disguise or protect itself in the Said, but it simply gives itself some words to the face of the Other.[40] Saying uncovers itself on its skin, that is, sensibility on the skin, and Saying offers itself onto suffering because of this sensibility, the nudity of the face of the Other.[41] Levinas writes a conclusive statement about Saying with the implication of substitution. "Substitution, at the limit of being, ends up in Saying, in the giving of sings, giving a sign of this giving of signs, expressing itself."[42]

In addition, proximity is a manifest foundation of human relationship, now that the signification to the other, responsibility, and Saying occurs in proximity. Proximity is very distinct from other human relationships because it "has to be conceived as a responsibility for the other."[43] Levinas elaborates that "being and entities weigh heavily by virtue of the saying that gives them light. Nothing is more grave, more august, than responsibility for the other, and saying, in which there is no play, has a gravity more grave than its own being or not being."[44] This relationship can be called "humanity, subjectivity, or self."[45] Peperzak explains this point:

> Saying, responsibility, goodness, proximity, subjectivity, inspiration, and spirituality do not fit into the horizons of kerygmatic discourse and logical appropriation. My own saying captures me

---

38. Ibid.
39. Levinas, "Essence and Disinterestedness," in *Basic Philosophical Writings*, 121.
40. Ibid.
41. Ibid.
42. Ibid.
43. Levinas, *Otherwise than Being*, 46.
44. Ibid.
45. Ibid.

in a movement that started before I could move my will. It takes me away from my attempt at identifying myself as the central or transcendental point of reference. The presentation of myself in my addressing words to someone cannot be welcomed within the system of *logos* and phenomenology. It cannot be gathered or synchronized within the said.[46]

Furthermore:

> To speak is not a special sort of intention that would be comparable to other noetico-noematic correlations; it is *transcendence*—the happening of a relation that "precedes" and conditions all sorts of intentions by offering the *whole* of my identifying and verbalizing acts, that is, the whole of my world, to someone who is not a part or moment or event within that whole. You and I are not to be found "*in*" the world, because you come afar and, in speaking to you, I do not coincide with my being-in-the-world.[47]

Thus, my beingness reveals in this human relationship in my *response-ability* to the Other. While the I *responds* to the face of the Other, my being becomes the initiative of my responsibility, not only for you and for all the others, but also for myself. While the I says to my neighbor with sincerity and frankness, my being is connected to the Other not because my subjectivity calls you and others to me as being-in-the-world, but because my response "precedes any nestling in the domain of phenomenal beings."[48] The phrase of "I *am* you, whenever I am I," thus, can be altered in this way: "I *respond to* you, whenever I am I," that is, it is my *response-ability* to say "here I am."

Asymmetry and the Human Reality

Based upon the phenomenological understanding of the face of the Other, Levinas develops his philosophical discourse into the realm of good and evil such as justice, resistance, peace, and equality. This is initiated by a new notion of human relation in Levinas, called, *asymmetry*, in terms of responsibility. According to Jeffrey Bloechl, Levinas signifies his philosophical

---

46. Peperzak, "Presentation," in Critchley and Bernasconi, *Re-reading Levinas*, 63.
47. Peperzak, *Beyond*, 66.
48. Ibid.

account of human responsibility in order to make human being discern good from evil.[49] Bloechl demonstrates that responsibility is radical in Levinas:

> The call to responsibility is already a call to justice, to care for many others at once. The competing appeals of my neighbor and the other Others literally give me pause: I must stop and reflect, think. And with this, the veritable birth of consciousness, my devotion to the absolute otherness reveling itself in my neighbor's face is already framed in language and phenomenality. True, that face will have exposed the innate pretentiousness of all words and appearances, but the fact that not one but many others claim my responsibility forces me to use them nonetheless. . . . Revolution will be necessary from time to time. The ethics of the other person claims to also be the political of that revolution.[50]

This radicality, however, does not originate by the traditional understanding of justice and equality which comes from the recognition of the subject-object relation or the subject-subject relation. Rather, it comes from the unconditional responsibility of the subject for the Other, that is, intersubjectivity, based on the new human relation, asymmetry.

For Levinas, ethical values, such as responsibility, obligation, equality, and justice, are revealed by the epiphany of the face. The epiphany of the face is fundamentally ethical. To begin with, the epiphany of the face of the Other makes the I join in the discourse, which has signification; simultaneously, the signification of the discourse is in the face of the Other, and all discourses take place within the primordial language of the face-to-face. Objectivity results from language, and language makes possible the objectivity of objects and their thematization.[51] Levinas says: "What I communicate therefore is already constituted in function of others. In speaking I do not transmit to the Other what is objective for me: the objective becomes objective only through communication."[52] Humanity relies on this discourse, that is, the epiphany of the face opens a person to the sense of equality through communication.[53] Here, the sense of justice makes a person recognize that there is a third party (*illeity*), which looks at me in

---

49. Bloechl, "Ethics as First Philosophy and Religion," in *The Face of the Other*, 143.
50. Ibid., 144. Bloechl explains that this idea comes from Levinas, *Entre Nous*, 229–31.
51. Levinas, *Totality and Infinity*, 206–10.
52. Ibid., 210.
53. Ibid., 213.

the eyes of the Other. It is language as a form of justice.[54] Discourse is not only the speech of the self setting forth an objective and common world, but also a sermon, an exhortation and the prophetic word:

> By essence the prophetic word responds to the epiphany of the face, doubles all discourse not as a discourse about moral themes, but as an irreducible movement of a discourse which by essence is aroused by the epiphany of the face inasmuch as it attests the presence of the third party, the whole humanity, in the eyes that look at me.[55]

Thus, Levinas's ethics starts not from some moral themes, but from the humanity whom the I meets. The relation with the Other and its discourse calls the I to be responsible and to have the sense of equality.[56] At this point, Levinas's thought about equality is noteworthy in that he considers *asymmetry* in human relation to be the basic way to create equality.[57] According to Levinas, symmetry creates a conditional human relation because it is founded on the give-and-take relationship. An unconditional relation, by contrast, is possible in asymmetry. Levinas demonstrates that "more, for my position as *I* consist in being able to respond to this essential destitution of the Other, finding resources for myself. The Other who dominates me in his transcendence is thus the stranger, the widow, and the orphan, to whom I am obligated."[58] Thus, equality is produced by my responsibility toward the Other. This relation is effectuated by the urgency with which the Other requires my response. This discourse urges justice and equality. That is, the face of the Other makes me responsible for the Other, and the Other joins in me during the discourse.

Proximity and responsibility make the I not only see the other as my neighbor, but also acknowledge that there is the third party around the I, as the main sources of justice and peace. The Other stands with the third party for whom the I may not completely answer any questions like, "What then are the other and the third party for one another? What have they done to one another? Which passes before the other?"[59] Distance among the I, the Other, and the third party is clear because of these questions. Levinas

---

54. Ibid., 212–14. See also Levinas, *Ethics and Infinity*, 89–90.
55. Levinas, *Totality and Infinity*, 213.
56. Ibid., 214.
57. Ibid., 215.
58. Ibid.
59. Levinas, *Otherwise than Being*, 157.

proposes the biblical rhetoric of Isaiah, "peace, peace to the neighbor and the one far-off" (Isa 57:19). This rhetoric becomes a very apparent matter to the self when the I asks the issue of justice, "What do I have to do with justice?"[60] This is the "question of consciousness," in that "justice is necessary, that is, comparison, coexistence, contemporaneousness, assembling, order, thematization, the visibility of faces, and thus intentionality and the intellect, and in intentionality and the intellect, the intelligibility of a system, and thence also a copresence on an equal footing as before a court of justice."[61] This is "the space of contiguity," that is, proximity. Proximity can be purely understood in this space, in Saying, and in responsibility because the question of consciousness can be answered in this space of contiguity.[62] Levinas explains: "In the proximity of the other, all the others and the other obsess me, and already this obsession cries out for justice, demands measure and knowing, is consciousness."[63] Thus, "the foundation of consciousness is justice," but not *vice versa*.[64] Because my neighbor, the third party, obsesses me with his or her face, the face and my relationship with the face makes the I envision the concern of justice:

> In proximity the other obsesses me according to the absolute asymmetry of signification, of the-one-for-the-other: I substitute myself for him, whereas no one can replace me, and the substitution of the one for the other does not signify the substitution of the other for the one. The relationship with the third party is an incessant correction of the asymmetry of proximity in which the face is looked at.[65]

Likewise, the issue of peace also has the same implication of justice in Levinas. Levinas demonstrates peace as the ethical relationship and the awakenness of the instability of the other, that is, the love for our neighbor in our proximity and responsibility.[66] Therefore:

> Consciousness is born as the presence of the third party in the proximity of the one for the other and, consequently, it is to the

---

60. Ibid.
61. Ibid.
62. Ibid., 157–58.
63. Ibid., 158. See also Levinas, "Peace and Proximity," in *Basic Philosophical Writings*, 169.
64. Levinas, *Otherwise than Being*, 160.
65. Ibid.
66. Levinas, "Peace and Proximity," 166–67.

extent that it proceeds from this that it can become dis-interestedness. The foundation of consciousness is justice and not the reverse. Objectivity reposing on justice. To the extravagant generosity of the for-the-other is superimposed a reasonable order, ancillary or angelic, of justice through knowledge, and philosophy here is a *measure* brought to the infinity of the being-for-the-other of peace and proximity, and is like the wisdom of love.[67]

The issue of justice and peace is based on my consciousness of the third party, which is a broadened concept of the Other, my neighbor, in responsibility and proximity, in that human relation is basically asymmetrical in front of the Infinity and the epiphany of the face of the Other.

Overall, Levinas answers the question of "why ethics?" such that the fundamental relationship of humanity is ethics, not because of my autonomous acknowledgment as the ethical-self, but because of the summon of the face of the Other and my obligation to respond to them. The "first philosophy" is ethics rather than ontology. Here, my *response-ability* to say "here I am" is not my ethical capability to do something good for others, but it is my passivity of all my actions through my recognition of my hostage status for others, that is, substitution. There is also the third party as my neighbors and more than my neighbors. The I can have consciousness of justice and peace because of this relationship between the I, the Other, and the third party. Ethics, as "first philosophy," thus, tells us that my beingness is obliged to respond, as the form of Saying, for the Other to the ethical questions like equality, justice, resistance, and peace. In the next part, I will explore another aspect of ethics and otherness through my examination of Kongzi's ethical thought of *ren* (human relatedness). Ironically, this strong point of ethics in Levinas reveals his weakness, since he does not fully expand his ethical thoughts to the realm of community and society in terms of ethics and otherness. In this sense, my exploration of Kongzi will illustrate another tenet of the ethics of otherness.

---

67. Ibid., 169. Levinas says that he modifies this phrase from *Otherwise than Being*, 159–61.

Part III

Confucius (Kongzi) and the *Analects*[1]

Now, I WILL READ the ancient Chinese tradition, focusing on Confucianism, as a contemporary scholarship in the study of ethics. The significance of this tradition is not only the issue of our comprehension of different cultures, but it is also the matter of our understanding of morality and ethics. To begin with, the dichotomy of Euro-American and East Asian will be used in this writing instead of Western/Eastern, because the traditional Western-Eastern dichotomy simplifies the international relations, and excludes other continents or countries. The Euro-American tradition is based on Christianity and the modern thoughts of the Enlightenment; whereas, the East Asian tradition is based on Confucianism, Buddhism, and Taoism. These days, these two traditions are mixed throughout the world in terms of a study of postmodernity and culture. Euro-American countries have been studying East Asian and Indian traditional religion and philosophy in order to study human-relatedness, and Asian countries are trying to study

---

1. "Confucius" is the Latinized name of Kongzi (BCE 551–479) given by the Euro-American society of the Jesuit missionaries, who were the first to call him "Confucius" in the seventeenth century. Kong Qui was his original name, but he was called Kongzi or Master Kong among his disciples. I will call him Kongzi instead of Confucius. However, if I need to refer to the tradition of Confucianism, I will use "Confucius," i.e., "Confucius tradition" or "Confucian ethics."

On the other hand, *The Confucius Analects* was translated first into Euro-American language also by the Jesuit missionaries, especially by Matteo Ricci. The English word *analects* means a selection which came from the Greek word *analekta*. The Chinese title of this book is *Lunyu*, which can be translated as "conversations." Thus, this book is a selection of conversations which was compiled by the later followers of Kongzi. I will call this book simply *The Analects* instead of *The Confucius Analects*.

I take this information from De Bary, *Sources of East Asian Tradition*, 1:29–30.

Part III: Confucius (Kongzi) and the Analects

the Euro-American tradition in order to find the method for industrializing and modernizing their countries. Thus, comprehension of the meaning of difference is one of the main goals in this part.

In this sense, a major criticism of the Confucian tradition from the Euro-American perspectives, including the modern East Asian scholarships which values the Euro-American tradition more, is that it supports patriarchy, oppressing women as it emphasizes the patriarchal value of family; and, it has also formulated a hierarchal social order as it values the imperial power.[2] Historically, Confucianism mainly occupied its ideological role for about two thousand years, from the *Han* dynasty (206 BCE) to the *Qing* dynasty (1911) in the mainland China. Scholars and rulers manipulated Confucianism to benefit the emperors and the male upper classes according to their ruling ideology. This ideology of classism and sexism affected the history of East Asian countries like Korea and Japan.[3] For instance, the ruling ideology of the *Chosun* dynasty of Korea, which is the last dynasty in Korea, was based on Neo-Confucianism, and the *Lee* regime had ruled the *Chosun* dynasty about five hundred years until at the early twentieth century. The Confucian tradition is embedded into Korean society even in contemporary democratic South Korea. On the one hand, many scholars criticize the Confucian tradition as I discussed above; on the other hand, some scholars argue that Korean society has to be tentative on the primitive Confucian interpretation of humanness rather than Confucian-"is" as the supporting ideology of the social system. My argument is also based on the latter discussion on the Confucian tradition, as the way how the primitive Confucian text interprets humanness and how it develops its own social values in terms of morality and ethics.

The morality and ethics of the Confucian tradition is categorized as virtue ethics in the Confucian four classics, such as the *Analects, Mencius (Mengzi), The Great Learning,* and *Book of Mean*. Those could be considered similar in concept to the Aristotelian ideas of self-cultivation, habituation, and the praxis of the virtues of humanity.[4] With this sense, those who appreciate the Confucian classics have studied these books to learn the ethical and moral significance of these sources, and to develop a comparative com-

---

2. Kang, "Confucian Familism," 168–189.

3. In order to see the historical background of Confucian tradition, see Yao, *Introduction to Confucianism,* and Fung, *Short History of Chinese Philosophy.*

4. Slingerland, "Virtue Ethics." Also see Aristotle, *Nicomachean Ethics,* and McIntyre, *After Virtue.*

prehension of both the Euro-American and East Asian traditions, not only of morality and ethics, but also of cultures and social contexts. Encounters with both cultures give us an assessment of Confucianism as situated in its social and cultural values, while stressing its ethical manifestation.

The first encounter of European Christianity with the Chinese traditions like Confucianism and Buddhism occurred when an Italian Jesuit missionary, Matteo Ricci (1552–1610), arrived in China in 1582. Ricci thought that he might have a dialogue with Buddhism as a relevant religion with Christianity, so that he listened to Buddhism and broaden Christian perspectives from it. As his dialogue with Buddhism went on, however, Ricci found its limitations and differences. Then, he began to pay attention to Confucianism and its texts, and accorded them with his high respect. He became friends with numerous Chinese scholars and officials, translated Confucian texts, and introduced these translations to Europe. Ricci's endeavor generated sinology among European enlightenment scholars like Voltaire, Leibniz, and Tindal. Gradually, sinology developed in the European countries and spread to America in the twentieth century. Jaspers, a French philosopher, was the forerunner of this study in Europe, and several scholars in the United States, like Wing-tsit Chan, Wm. T. de Bary, Tu Weiming, Cheng Chung-ying, Roger T. Ames, and Rodney L. Taylor, led the way into the texts and contexts of the Confucian traditions. Their influences have been enormous, not only for the study of sinology, *per se*, but also for research in the fields of politics, ethics and culture.[5] This encounter with different cultures has encouraged the development of various fields of scholarships to study identity, diversity, difference, community, for both Euro-American and East Asian societies.

The interpretation of ethics and morality is one of the major topics of contemporary scholarship in sinology. Confucian philosophy and ethics values moral character more than moral acts. This does not mean that the Confucian tradition ignores righteous moral acts, but it means that this tradition counts more on the moral agency and the moral characteristics of this agency like virtues, goodness, benevolence, and propriety. These characteristics are the basis for becoming the exemplary person (*junzi*) *in and for* the society.[6] For instance, Chenyang Li exemplifies the term of *ren/jen* as the starting point of his discernment of Confucian ethics in a feminist

---

5. Yao, *Introduction to Confucianism*, introduction, 1–15.
6. Lau, trans., *Confucius—The Analects*, intro (italics mine).

interpretation, "the feminist ethics of care."⁷ Although *ren* was mentioned more than a hundred times in the *Analects*, there is no formal definition of *ren* in the Confucian tradition. Li focuses on two senses in the term *ren*, a "*ren* of affection," and a "*ren* of virtue." The former speaks of the "tenderness or altruistic care for others," and the latter does "a prefect or culminating virtue."⁸ Nyitray recapitulates:

> Li more or less maintains the traditional view: *jen*-affection is experienced from childhood in a home, the locus for one's moral training'; the more encompassing *jen*-virute is both cultivated and manifested in the performance of responsibilities and obligations of the Five Relationships—ruler-minister, father-son, husband-wife, older brother-younger brother, and friends—as outlined in *Mencius* 3A4. The ultimate goal of Confucius self-cultivation is to perfect and manifest *jen* in all one's relationships. Li finds similarities between *jen*, the goal of Confucius ethics, and the notion of care and sets out to build his case that classical Confucianism is comparable to "the feminist ethics of care." Care ethics posits that female modes of moral interaction and decision making are relational, flexible, attentive to the needs of the other, and find concrete expression in "care" for the other.⁹

This interpretation of Confucian ethics defines the implication of moral character in terms of human relatedness and care for the other. This comprehension of Confucian ethics is beneficial for the study of the Chinese tradition from both the Euro-American and East Asian viewpoints.

More specifically, the study of the Confucian tradition is the issue of identity and humanness in terms of ethics and morality in the Confucian tradition. I will concentrate on the primitive Confucianism, in particular, on one of the primitive Confucian texts,¹⁰ *The Analects*, in order to develop

---

7. Nyitray, "Confusion, Elision, and Erasure." Nyitray's writing about Li is based on Li's article "The Confucian Concept of *Jen* and the Feminist Ethics of Care," in Li's *The Sage and the Second Sex*.

8. Nyitray, "Confusion, Elision, and Erasure," 151.

9. Ibid., 151–52.

10. Yao explains the three periods theory to explore the historical grounds of Confucianism according to a modern Confucian philosopher, Mou Zongsan (1908–95). Yao writes, "The first epoch from Confucius (551–479 BCE), Mengzi (371–289 BCE) and Xunzi (310?-211? BCE) to Dong Zhongshu represents the origin of Confucianism and the acceptance of the tradition as the mainstream ideology, which corresponds to the period from the Spring and Autumn period (770–476 BCE) to the end of the Later *Han* Dynasty (25–220). The second epoch starts from the renaissance of Neo-Confucianism and

my argument of the issue of humanness in Confucian ethics. One of the common misunderstandings about primitive Confucianism is that it does not guarantee individuality or the sense of the autonomous self, but it demands total altruism and sacrifice of the self to the other. Another common criticism is that Confucianism does not fit in a democratic society, in that it focuses on the East Asian communitarianism which is based on the bloodline familial relationship, making the society very hierarchical. Confucian ethics, therefore, has been interpreted as very authoritarian and hierarchical that it is their burden in their lifetime.[11] These misunderstandings came from a different understanding of humanity in the Euro-American tradition, which is ontological as it focuses on human subjectivity or intersubjectivity. The East Asian tradition is relational since it focuses on human relatedness. These two traditions seem to be opposed to each other because of their different foci on anthropology. Both traditions, however, have a common ground of ethics that is the concern of humanity and selfhood. With this implication, I will demonstrate how the East Asian tradition, in particular, one of the primitive Confucius texts, the *Confucius Analects*, acknowledges selfhood and its ethical foci.[12] I will explore the significance

---

its spread to the other parts of East Asia and ends with the abolition of the dominance of Confucianism in China and East Asia, corresponding to the era from the *Song* Dynasty (960-1279) to the beginning of the twentieth century. The third epoch takes place in the twentieth century, beginning with the critical reflection on the tradition initiated in the May Fourth Movement (1919) and which is still an ongoing process. A significant feature of the third epoch is that modern Confucian scholars propagate and reinterpret Confucian doctrines in the light of Western traditions, in which Confucianism is being brought into the world and the world into Confucianism." This term, "primitive Confucianism" is an academic term to explain the time period of Confucianism which matches the first period of the three periods theory. Primitive Confucianism, however, is not exactly fit in the three periods theory in that it tells of a more original form of Confucianism as Christian tradition finds the original texts as its primitive texts. Thus, scholars usually deal with the three texts as the primitive texts of Confucianism such as the *Analects*, *Mencius*, and *Xunzi*. On the other hand, the four books of Confucianism, the *Analects*, *Mencius*, *Book of Mean*, and *the Great Learning*, were canonized by Zhu Xi (1139-1193), the great scholar of Neo-Confucianism.

11. Interestingly, these criticisms are not original in this contemporary era, but are from the ancient era. Several ancient philosophers in ancient China, especially Mo Tzu, criticized Kongzi as a hypocrite in that he does not tell universal love for the self, but it sees only the outlook of the personality in terms of propriety.

12. There are several English translations of *The Analects*. As I discussed above, Matteo Ricci translated it first, and another missionary, James Legge (1815-1897), translated the four books into English. Legge's translations are considered as the first modern English version of the Chinese classics. Recently, several scholars translated them again

of *ren*, demonstrating that Confucianism is based on the notion of human relatedness in order to achieve the fulfillment of humanity; it has its own ethical significance as it developed the idea of self-cultivation for humanness; and it has an ultimate goal to build an ideal society as it pursues *ren* according to the foundation of *tao* (the Way).

---

according to the new scholarships of sinology, such as D. C. Lau (1979), Roger T. Ames and Henry Rosemont Jr. (1998), E. Bruce Brooks and A. Taeko Brooks (1998), and Edward Slingerland (2003). Brooks reorganized *The Analects* based on historical and literature criticism (they published this, titled *The Original Analects*), and Slingerland added several commentaries related to the old and new commentaries, like Dong Zhongshu, Zhu Xi and other commentators. I will mainly refer to Slingerland, *Confucius Analects*, as I designate this simply *"The Analects"* in this writing, and if necessary, I will refer to other translations.

Chapter 5

Ren and Humanness

REN IS NOT ONLY the source of life, but also it is the foundation of ethics and morality in Kongzi, as it is the keystone of the conception of humanness. In this section, I will explore three points of Kongzi's life and teaching: What kind of person Kongzi wanted to be, not only for himself, but also for his disciples and others; what the main topic of his teaching is; and why Kongzi values *ren* through his lifetime. I will demonstrate that *ren* is the crux of Kongzi's philosophical thought as I delve into three key words, *junzi*, *tao*, and *ren* in *The Analects*.

Kongzi and *Junzi*

In the first passage of *The Analects*, Kongzi articulates the three joyful moment of *junzi*: "To learn and then have occasion to practice what you have learned—is this not satisfying? To have friends arrive from afar—is this not a joy? To be patient even when others do not understand—is this not the mark of the gentlemen (*junzi*)?"[1] This passage shows us what the main ideas of *The Analects* are: learning and practicing through self-cultivation, thinking of others, and the right attitude in human relation. This passage tells us how Kongzi develops his anthropological philosophy and what he explores during his lifetime in order to build an ideal human relationship. This is also the foundation of the fiduciary community, i.e., family, a local community, and a state or a nation. The main goal of Kongzi's philosophy is to reevaluate the traditions of the Sage Kings in ancient China and to

---

1. Slingerland, trans., *Confucius Analects*, 1, book 1:1 (parenthesis is mine).

reformulate these traditions into his contemporary society. In this sense, Kongzi says himself, "I transmit rather than innovate. I trust in and love the ancient ways."[2]

What Kongzi wants to transmit is the Way (*tao*) of the culture of the legendary Sage Kings.[3] *Junzi* is the exemplary person who follows the Way, which is translated as "gentleman," "authoritative person," "superior man," "noble person," and also "exemplary person." The original meaning of the term *junzi* is "son of a lord,"[4] but, there is no exact definition of *junzi* in *The Analects*; instead, Kongzi explains *junzi* in his narratives and examples. As I cited the first passage of *The Analects* above, *junzi*'s joyful moment is to follow the great examples of "the ancient ways" which is found in human relation.[5] *Junzi* does not enjoy the temporal moment of a transcendental instant of religion, nor an ephemeral pleasure of humanity. Kongzi teaches:

> The gentleman is not motivated by the desire for a full belly or a comfortable abode. He is simply scrupulous in behavior and careful in speech, drawing near to those who possess the Way in order to be set straight by them. Surely this and nothing else is what it means to love learning.[6]

---

2. *Analects*, 64, book 7:1.

3. The Way (*tao*) is mentioned about eighty times in *The Analects*. It is not only the main idea of Confucianism, but it also is significant to Taoism.

The etymological approach of *tao* has two basic meanings, *chou*, "to pass over," or "to lead through," and *shou*, "head," or "foremost." The earliest appearance of this term *tao* was in the *Book of Documents* which meant "leading" an overflowing river through its banks.

Tao, thus, has both simultaneous meanings of physical and metaphorical, "road, path, way," and "method, art, teaching." In *The Analects*, the Way is to follow and experience the way of the cultural predecessors, and to provide the road map and direction for the cultural successors.

See also the introduction of Ames and Rosemont's translation of the *Analects*, 45. Also see Hall and Ames, *Thinking through Confucius*, 226–31.

4. De Bary, *Sources of East Asian Tradition*, 1:30.

5. Mengzi's commentary of the three joys of the gentleman tells also these features more specifically. "A gentleman takes joy in three things, and being king of the world is not one of them. His first joy is that his parents are both alive and his siblings have no difficulties. His second joy is that looking up he is not disgraced before Heaven, and looking down he is not ashamed before humans. His third joy is getting the assistance of and cultivating the brave and talented people of the world. The gentleman takes joy in three things, and being King of the world is not one of them." Van Norden, trans., *Mengzi*, 176, book 7A1, 2, 3, 4, 5.

6. *Analects*, 6, book 1:14.

Ren and Humanness

Truly, the Way does not bring physical comforts or desires for the human being, but it makes people live a straightforward life in establishing human behaviors such as daily speech, postures, and even dining manners. The Way makes people engage in self-cultivation through their lifetime learning process in order to follow it. Kongzi also values religious rituals as a source of this straightforward attitude toward life as the process of pursuing the Way rather than as a special transcendental experience of humanity. Kongzi refers to the existence of ghosts (*gui*) and spirits (*shen*) several times in the *Analects*, but he is not concerned with the religious meaning of them that have such transcendental power that people should adore them unconditionally. Rather, Kongzi is basically concerned with the right ritual rather than serving ghosts or spirits, as he teaches the right sacrifice:

> To sacrifice to spirits that are not one's own is to be presumptuous. To see what is right, but to fail to do it, is to be lacking in courage.[7]
>
> "Sacrifice as if [they were] present" means that, when sacrificing to the spirits, you should comport yourself as if the spirits were present. If I am not fully present at the sacrifice, it is as if I did not sacrifice at all.[8]

A sincere attitude toward the ritual, thus, is a basis for humanity. Kongzi values this attitude more such as, "working to ensure social harmony among the common people, respecting the ghosts and spirits while keeping them at a distance—this might be called wisdom."[9] Respect and distance is the root of the sacrifice and ritual, such that Kongzi's locus of ritual is based on the formulation of harmony among people instead of a superficial sacrifice for spirits in order to have a sense of security. The fundamental idea of sacrifice to the spirits, thus, is to serve people rather than to serve the spirit itself.[10]

The Way is not an optional norm of human action, but it is the ultimate concern for *junzi*. Kongzi's ultimacy and his resoluteness toward the Way are shown in the *Analects*, as he says, "having in the morning heard that the Way was being put into practice, I could die that evening without regret,"[11] and "the gentleman (*junzi*) devotes his thoughts to attaining the Way, not

---

7. Ibid., 16, book 2:24.
8. Ibid., 21, book 3:12.
9. Ibid., 60, book 6:22.
10. Ibid., 115, book 11:12.
11. Ibid., 32, book 4:8.

to obtaining food. In the pursuit of agriculture, there is the possibility of starvation; in the pursuit of learning, there is the possibility of salary. The gentleman is concerned about the Way and not about poverty."[12] Poverty or even death cannot become any hindrance to follow the Way. The Way cannot be accomplished in a moment at all, but it is a lifelong process which humans should learn and practice sincerely in order to reach the Way as a *junzi*.

> Whose disciples will be the first to be taught the Way of the gentleman, and then in the end grow tired of it? It is like the grass and the trees: you make distinctions between them according to their kind. The Way of gentleman, how can it be slandered so? Starting at the beginning and working through to the end—surely this describes none other than the sage![13]

Finally, humans can reach Goodness (*ren*), which is the ultimate concern of *junzi* in order to fulfill humanity; then, life and death cannot divide the Way for *junzi*. Kongzi articulates this stage of humanity in this way: "No scholar-official of noble intention or Good person would ever pursue life at the expense of Goodness, and in fact some may be called upon to give up their lives in order to fulfill Goodness."[14] The Way inspires humanity to live in goodness, not because they can get their existence from the Way, but because only the Way drives them to life, and even to death.

In addition, *junzi* practices Virtue (*de*) in order to follow the Way. In Confucianism, the word virtue is usually capitalized as "Virtue" (*de*) in order to show its uniqueness like the Way (*tao*), and the Heavenly Mandate (*tien-ming*). Virtue has its uniqueness in that it not only reveals humanity (benevolence, *ren*), but it also practices unceasingly the Way according to the Heavenly Mandate. Virtue bases its ongoing practice on effortless action (*wu-wei*). Virtue is also a kind of charismatic power in order to follow the Way of the great Sage Kings like Yao and Shun as they resided in the Way of the Heavenly Mandate with the ruling power of effortless action.[15] With

12. Ibid., 187, book 15:32 (parenthesis is mine).
13. Ibid., 225, book 19:12.
14. Ibid., 177, book 15:9.

15. On the contrary, the concept of virtue in the Euro-American tradition signifies the right action of a particular work in order to foster others according to its right direction. According to Aristotle, it is a pattern of human action which is obtained by practice in the way that humans usually tend to act. Thomas Aquinas explains that virtue is habit that illustrates the perfection of human power in action. In the medieval church tradition, there were four *cardinal virtues*, temperance, courage, prudence, and justice, which Christians live, learn, and practice. Virtue is based not only on the cultural backgrounds

this sense, *junzi* does not practice Virtue with a visual or artificial method in order to show something outwardly, but he or she can and must reveal the Way as they practice Virtue in their everyday life. Kongzi exemplifies this practice of Virtue with "effortless action" (*wu-wei*) and "timely action." For instance, when Kongzi achieves a public position, he acts respectfully and thoughtfully toward others; when he goes to the ancestral temples, he speaks eloquently; he would not eat excessively even if he has enough good food in his hands;[16] and he avoids four faults: arbitrariness, inflexibility, rigidity, and selfishness.[17] Kongzi provides a great example of timeliness and effortlessness in *The Analects*:

> Those men who went into seclusion include Bo Yi, Shu Qi, Yu Zhong, Yi Yi, Zhu Zhang, Liuzia Hui, and Shao Lian.
> The Master said, "Unwilling to lower their aspirations or bring disgrace upon their persons—such were Bo Yi and Shu Qi."
> Of Liuxia Hui and Shao Lian he said, "Although they lowered their aspirations and brought disgrace upon their persons, at least their speech was in accord with their status and their actions were in accord with their thoughts."
> Of Yu Zhong and Yi Yi he said, "Living in seclusion and freely speaking their minds, their persons remained pure and their resignations from office were well-considered."
> He concluded, "I, however, am different from all of them in that I have no preconceived notions of what is permissible and what is not."[18]

These three examples show us the different attitudes of life after they were expelled from their loyal positions. They kept their dignity as the followers of the Way as they responded to their situations in the Way as timely as they

---

which are so different in values depending on a particular action that the community narrative signifies in virtue, but it is also based on the universal virtues like kindness, hospitality, honesty, and so on (Lovin, *Christian Ethics*, ch. 4). The difference of both traditions in virtue is the method of obtaining and revealing of the virtues. Kongzi taught that Virtue is to follow the great exemplary Sages with effortless action; whereas, the Western tradition focuses on the learning and practicing of virtues in order to obtain them.

I will discuss more about this aspect in section three of this chapter and the next chapter of this writing as I explore the ethical features of *The Analects*, and as I do comparative study between Levinas and Kongzi.

16. *Analects*, 98–99, 103, book 10:1, 2, 8.
17. Ibid., 87, book 9:4.
18. Ibid., 219, book 18:8.

could.[19] The concrete action is not separated from our everydayness, but it is directly related to our communal life in our everydayness. Therefore, humans do not have to practice virtues as they exaggerate themselves to others; rather, people have to endeavor to do everything as effortlessly as they value timeliness for every situation. Also, it does not mean that people need to change their attitudes according to the vicissitude of their situations. Yet, it means that they can live their life with majesty as they follow true Virtue through practicing and learning of it. That is the Way that *junzi* enjoys his or her everyday life.

The Way (*Tao*) and *Ren*

The term *ren* appears 105 times, in 58 sections out of the total 499 sections in the *Analects*. This term appeared rarely in the earliest Chinese classics in ancient China like *Book of Songs*, *Book of History*, *Book of Change (I-Ching)*, *Book of Rites*, and *The Spring and Autumn Annals*, which Kongzi valued as his canons. Kongzi, however, mentioned it exceptionally many times in the *Analects*, so that *ren* is the main idea of Kongzi and Confucianism. The etymological explanation of this term has two elements in it, *ren* (both words are pronounced the same) "person," and *er*, the number "two." The basic understanding of this word is one cannot become a person by oneself, that means that originally people are "we." *Ren* is commonly translated into "benevolence," "goodness," "humanity," "humanheartedness," "humanness," and "authoritative conduct." These translations reveal how this term is important, but it is not fully understood at a glance. Yet, the common sense of this term is that it values humanity and the sense of community as it examines the significance of human relatedness.[20] This etymological understanding of *ren*, human relatedness, is the main key to understand the conception of the Way in Kongzi.

To begin with, the Way does not rely on a distinctively speculative theory, but it explains the consistency, steadiness, and sincerity in our lives. We can explore the Way in the narratives of Kongzi with his disciples. The

---

19. See also *Mengzi*, 131, book 5B1. In *Mengzi*, we can read same anecdotes with some more detailed information.

20. "Introduction," in Ames and Rosemont, trans., *Analects*, 48–51. Also see Hall and Ames, *Thinking through Confucius*, 110–30.
The meaning of "humanity," "humanness," or "human relatedness" is mainly discussed in this writing as I follow the etymological interpretation of *ren*. If necessary, I will refer to other translations in this writing in order to clarify of each contextual meanings of *ren*.

Ren and Humanness

Way is also based on the narrative of Kongzi about *ren*. Kongzi says, "All that I teach can be strung together on a single thread."[21] He says again, almost identically, that "I bind it all together with a single thread."[22] The original Chinese text is written "all that I teach" as "my Way (*tao*)," thus, this sentence can be interpreted as Kongzi's consistent attitude toward the Way, which he wants to teach as a consistency to his disciples. The core of the Way is *ren*, not only the basis of humanness, but also as the foundation of the Way which *junzi* follows, as he or she practices right Virtue. Kongzi argues:

> Wealth and social eminence are things that all people desire, and yet unless they are acquired in the power way I will not abide them. Poverty and disgrace are things that all people hate, and yet unless they are avoided in the power of way I will not despise them.
>
> If the gentleman (*junzi*) abandons Goodness (*ren*), how can he merit the name? The gentleman does not go against Goodness even for the amount of time required to finish a meal. Even in times of urgency or distress, he necessarily accords with it.[23]

This attitude toward *ren* in terms of the Way exactly corresponds to what Kongzi was saying, that "to live in the neighborhood of the Good (*ren*) is fine,"[24] "those who are Good feel at home in Goodness (*ren*),"[25] and again, "having in the morning heard that the Way was being put into practice, I could die that evening without regret."[26] The Way, thus, has its foundation in Kongzi's teaching about *ren*.

---

21. *Analects*, 34, book 4:15.

22 According to *The Analects*, Kongzi taught this to his pupil Zeng. Zeng commented on this to his disciples, that "all that the Master teaches amounts to nothing more than dutifulness (*zhong*) and tempered by understanding (*shu*)" (*Analects*, 34, book 4:15). Van Norden wrote an article, "Unweaving the 'One Thread' of Analects 4:15," in *Confucius and the* Analects, 216–36. Van Norden tried to find the features of *zhong* and *shu* as he explored what Kongzi's one thread was in this article. I will develop my argument that *zhong* and *shu* are among the main characters of *ren* in my writing in the next two chapters, as I explore the features of *ren* in terms of the study of intersubjectivity and ethics. In this section, I will focus more on *ren* as "the one thread" of Kongzi related to the study of the Way. Ibid., 174, book 15:3.

23. Ibid., 31, book 4:5 (parenthesis is mine).

24. Ibid., 29, book 4:1 (parenthesis is mine).

25. Ibid, book 4:2 (parenthesis is mine).

26. Ibid., 32, book 4:8.

The Way is the lifelong process of humanity to accomplish *ren* and to change the world.[27] Kongzi teaches, "No Scholar-official of noble intention or Good person would ever pursue life at the expense of Goodness (*ren*), and in fact some may be called upon to give up their lives in order to fulfill Goodness (*ren*)."[28] Thus, the Way of life-giving for the world is such that sacrificial love can make humans realize the significance of humanity in terms of Goodness (*ren*). To follow the Way, without ignoring humanity, comes from the realization of the Goodness (*ren*). The Way is accomplished by the life-giving resoluteness of humanity for it. Kongzi articulates that "human beings can broaden the Way—it is not the Way that broadens human beings."[29] According to commentaries on this passage, we can find the basic tenet of the Way that it is manifested in its full realization by human being, and this realization is the principle that the Way is transcendent of the sense of the world.[30] Yet, the Way is not an unconditional pursuit of the impossible things which a person cannot follow, but it is the ongoing process of fulfilling the Goodness (*ren*). Human beings can reach the Way through the fulfillment of Goodness (*ren*), i.e., the Way of humanity making and changing the world *within and through ren*.

For instance, Kongzi teaches a very practical way to fulfill *ren*, saying that "restraining yourself and returning to the rites constitutes Goodness (*keji fuli*). The key to achieving Goodness lies within yourself—how could it come from other?"[31] The Confucian concept of ritual has a different understanding of other religious rituals in the Euro-American tradition, in that *li* (rites) is related to the propriety of human relationships, i.e., between emperor and subjects, between parents and children, between husband and wife, between teacher and students, and between the older and the younger.[32] In this sense, ritual is very critical in human relationship because humanity can be revealed while people practice various rituals. The Goodness of humanity, however, does not belong to any particular rite; rather, rituals belong to humanity. Kongzi points this out very clearly with the very similar notion of the golden rule in the Gospels in Christianity: "Do not

---

27. Hall and Ames, *Thinking through Confucius*, 229–30.
28. *Analects*, 177, book 15:9 (parenthesis is mine).
29. Ibid., 185–86, book 15:29.
30. Ibid.
31. Ibid., 125, book 12:1.
32. Kongzi did not categorize these human relations explicitly in the *Analects*. Instead, Mengzi develops these categories. See *Mengzi*, 70–71, book 3A4.

impose upon others what you yourself do not desire.... When in public, comport yourself as if you were receiving an important guest, and in your management of the common people, behave as if you were overseeing a great sacrifice."[33] The Way of self-sacrifice in order to return to the rites (*li*), thus, is an important example of showing us the Way for the accomplishment of *ren*.

In addition, there is another basis to understand the Way, that is, the Way of the Heavenly mandate (*tian-ming*), related to the interpretation of the generation of the world in harmony and equilibrium. According to *Book of Mean*, Kongzi explains the idea of harmony and equilibrium:

> What Heaven imparts to man is called human nature. To follow our nature is called the Way (*tao*). Cultivating the Way is called education.... Before the feelings of pleasure, anger, sorrow, and joy are aroused it is called equilibrium (*chung*, centrality, mean). When these feelings are aroused and each and all attain due measure and degree, it is called harmony. Equilibrium is the great foundation of the world, and harmony its universal path. When equilibrium and harmony are realized to the highest degree, heaven and earth will attain their proper order and all things will flourish.[34]

Kongzi mentions *zhong-yong* (the principle of mean) once in the *Analects*, as follows: "Acquiring Virtue by applying the mean—is this not best? And yet among the common people few are able to practice this virtue for long."[35] With this sense of *zhong-yong*, Kongzi develops his idea of *tien-ming* in his conception of Virtue and the notion of harmony and equilibrium.

Generally, *tian* is translated as heaven, and *ming* as life and death, fate, or mandate. Yet, *tian* is usually understood as the basis of moral principles, and as nature itself.[36] *Ming* is understood as "life and death"; whereas, *ming* replaces sometimes the word *tian-ming* in *The Analects*.[37] For instance, Kongzi says, "One who does not understand fate (*ming*) lacks the means to become a gentleman (*junzi*)."[38] In this sense, Kongzi instructs that *junzi* has to follow the Heavenly Mandate as he teaches three things that *junzi* has to

---

33. Ibid., 126, book 12:2.

34. Chan, trans., "The Doctrine of Mean," in *Source Book in Chinese Philosophy*, 98. *Chung* is the same pronunciation of *zhong*.

35. *Analects*, 63, book 6:29.

36. Yao, *Introduction to Confucianism*, 147–53.

37. See *Analects*, book 6:10, 11:18, 12:5, 14:36, 19:1, 20:3.

38. Ibid., 235, book 20:3 (parenthesis is mine).

stand in awe: the Mandate of Heaven, great men, and the teachings of the sages.³⁹ In addition, *tian-ming* is the foundation of his ultimate concern of the Way as he focuses on his life path as he receives his life from the Heaven (*tian*), following the Way of *tian*. Kongzi claims, "At fifty, I understood Heaven's Mandate,"⁴⁰ and he says, "It is Heaven itself that has endowed me with virtue."⁴¹ Kongzi exemplifies this point as he teaches that his teaching came from Heaven, to which his disciples had and still have to listen:

> The Master sighed, "Would that I did not have to speak!"
> Zigong said, "If the Master did not speak, then how would we little ones receive guidance from you?"
> The Master replied, "What does Heaven ever say? Yet the four seasons are put in motion by it, and the myriad creatures receive their life from it. What does Heaven ever say?"⁴²

Tian is the foundation of the world, heaven and earth, as well as the Way which humans follow.

Hall and Ames demonstrate the Way of *tian-ming* as they explain the relations between individual (*ren*) and Heaven (*tian*):

> The problem of the relation between *t'ien ming* and *ming* might be solved in such a manner as this: the individual who has attained a high degree of integration of the sort associated with the exemplary person (*chun tzu*) or the sage (*sheng jen*) has established a peculiarly immanent relationship with *t'ien* which permits him access to the *ming* of *t'ien* both in terms of understanding and of influence. The less intensely focused an individual is, the greater is his sense of *ming* as determining conditions over which he seems to exercise no control; the more intensely focused he is, the greater is his awareness of the role he can play in determining those conditions. Where the world defers to his excellence, he "speaks" for the world; that is, he speaks for *t'ien*.⁴³

Thus, the Way of Heaven is a continuous process of understanding the world and the human being, as Kongzi emphasizes that his Way came from the Heavenly Mandate (*tian-ming*). Namely, the Way is to follow the

---

39. Ibid., 195, book 16:8.
40. Ibid., 9, book 2:4.
41. Ibid., 71, book 7:23.
42. *Analects*, 208, book 17:19.
43. Hall and Ames, *Thinking through Confucius*, 215. T'ien equals *tian*, and *chun tzu* equals *junzi*.

Heavenly Mandate in order to fulfill *ren* for humanity.[44] The Way is the foundation of humanity in the world, and the one that people have to walk all the time. Life and death cannot be divided because of the Way. The Way inspires people to live in *ren*, not only because a person gets his or her life from the Way, but also because a person can give up his or her life for *ren* in order to pursue the Way. The finality of humanity, thus, is to reach *ren*, that is, the ultimate concern of humanity in Kongzi.

Ren and Humanness

Wing-Tsit Chan categorizes the tenets of *ren* according to the Confucian tradition from the primitive period to the Neo-Confucian period: virtue as the basis of ethics, love as universal law, all human beings as the foundation of the universe, the active and dynamic relationship among people as well as between people and nature, the foundation of goodness, and the source of transcendence and metaphysics.[45] Except for the last category which Neo-Confucianism formulated as it tried to turn Confucianism into a religious category,[46] the other categories demonstrate the ethical manifestation of the relationality and the sociality of humanity. Hall and Ames signifies this aspect of *ren* as the root of humanness, with *ren* as a process of "qualitative transformation of the person and achievement of authoritative humanity," that is, "person making."[47] This is not an inner psychic understanding of the individual self, but it is an outer/active engagement of people toward others and the world.[48] This person making process, as one of the main ideas of *ren*, inspires people to follow the Way in order to be an authoritative and exemplary person (*junzi*).[49] *Ren*, thus, is the most important concept related to Kongzi's comprehension of humanness as it is not only the *origin* of humanity, but it is also the *telos* of the human being.

44. In order to see more features about the Heavenly Mandate, also see *Mengzi*, 171, book 7A1, 2

45. Chan, "The Evolution of the Confucian Concept of *Jen*," *Philosophy East and West*, 295–319. *Jen* is the same as *ren*.

46. In order to discuss of the religious aspect of Nee-Confucianism, see *Short History of Chinese Philosophy*, esp. chs. 23–25.

47. Hall and Ames, *Thinking through Confucius*, 114–15.

48. Fingarette, *Confucius*, ch. 3. Fingarette emphasized *li* (participation in rituals) as the embodiment of *ren* in this book. I will discuss this feature of *li* and *ren* in terms of human relatedness and intersubjectivity in the next section.

49. Hall and Ames, *Thinking through Confucius*, 115.

Making people is not only the way that the human being becomes the moral self to follow and practice the Way, but also the way that humanity values his or her relatedness in terms of the acknowledgment of otherness. As I discussed above, the etymological approach of *ren* is based on human relatedness, as *ren*, in itself, came from the acceptance and reliance of others. This is the reason why *ren* is translated as human heartedness, Goodness, benevolence, authoritative action, human relatedness, and humanness. With these senses, there are two crucial points of *ren*; the goodness of humanity (*ren*) as the basis of virtue, and the foundation of human action in terms of human relation. In other words, *ren* is not a simple virtue of humanity to become a good person like benevolence; rather, it is the basis of human relation. In particular, it is the foundation of human public life related to morality and ethics. Here is the paradox of *ren* that the goodness of humanity is not based on the acknowledgment of the individual self as the center of humanity, but it is on the openness of the self to others. As I already mentioned, Kongzi explains this aspect when one of his disciples, Yan Hui, asked about Goodness (*ren*):

> Restraining yourself and returning to the rite constitutes Goodness (*keji fuli*). If for one day you managed to restrain yourself and return to the rites, in this way you could lead the entire world back to Goodness. The key to achieving Goodness lies within yourself—how could it come from others?[50]

And Kongzi specifies more:

> Do not look unless it is in accordance with ritual; do not listen unless it is in accordance with ritual; do not speak unless it is in accordance with ritual; do not move unless it is in accordance with ritual.[51]

These details: looking, listening, speaking and moving, are the actions of the individual self; yet, those are the basis of communal life. Thus, the self can engage himself or herself into the goodness of humanity through the way of self-restraint and ritual propriety so that people watch out for themselves before they try to achieve goodness for themselves.

Kongzi develops how we can be familiar with *ren*, as he asks, "Is really Goodness so far away?" Then, he answers, "If I simply desire Goodness, I will find that it is already here."[52] It is the paradox of *ren* that *ren* is *already*

---

50. Ibid., 125, book 12:1.
51. Ibid.
52. *Analects*, 74, book 7: 30.

in us, but *not yet* since it comes to us only when we desire it. This means that we have to simplify ourselves for others according to *ren* in order to overcome our self-centeredness. This is also the way of happiness. Kongzi says more, "To live in the neighborhood of the Good (*ren*) is fine. If one does not choose to dwell among those who are Good, how will one obtain wisdom" and "without Goodenss (*ren*), one cannot remain constant in adversity and cannot enjoy enduring happiness."[53] These two sentences demonstrate the consistent attitude of Kongzi for *ren*. *Ren* makes people not only experience happiness even if they are in difficulties, but also reside with good neighbors, that is, the wisdom of life. Also, this is the wisdom of *ren*. Namely, this wisdom makes human being obtain *the* sense of true love that "only one who is Good is able to truly love others or despise others."[54] True love does not mean that humans should love others with an unlimited benevolent action like total altruism, but it means that people need to love others impartially and accurately. People should not only be free from their bad intentions toward others in order to attain impartial *ren*,[55] but they should also hate a lack of *ren* in order to truly love *ren*.[56] This is *the* wisdom of *ren*, which makes people love *ren*, and then, makes people enjoy their life in *ren* as they become blissful because of the impartiality of love.

Ren is not a self-centered love but it is the love to others through the awareness of otherness in *ren*.[57] When Fan Chi asked about *ren*, Kongzi answered that Goodness is to "care for others." Then, Fan Chi asked about wisdom, and Kongzi replied, "Know others."[58] There is a little difference of translation in Slingerland from the original Chinese text. The word "care" in the translation of Slingerland is originally understood as "love." Yet, Slingerland translates this as "care" that he insightfully catches the original textual meaning from the *Analects*, since "love" is not a simple mind-set of humanity; rather, it is the concrete moral motivation of humans, that is, "care." Kongzi emphasizes the five ways of *ren* in terms of "care." Kongzi explains, "Someone could be considered Good who is able to, everywhere in the world, put five virtues into practice"—"reverence, magnanimity, trustworthiness, diligence, and kindness." He explicates:

53. Ibid., 29, book 4:1 and 2.
54. Ibid., 30, book 4:3.
55. Ibid, book 4:4.
56. Ibid., 31, book 4:6.
57. Ibid., 37, book 4:25.
58. Ibid., 136, book 12:22.

> If you are reverent, you will avoid disgrace; if you are magnanimous, you will win the populace; if you are trustworthy, others will put their trust in you; if you are diligent, you will achieve results; and if you are kind, you will have the wherewithal to employ the people.[59]

Thus, "care" does not simply mean to love others with an altruistic perspective; rather, it means that humans should keep their virtues. This is the best way to discipline the self and go forth to the ritual in order to "care" for others. Namely, the self cannot live a virtuous life without *ren*, the love to others.

Lastly, Hall and Ames develop the conception of *ren* and humanity, as they demonstrate that the relation between the self and the other in the *Analects* is the "relational self."[60] This illustration of human relation legitimately explains the concept of selfhood in the *Analects*, as compared with that of Euro-American philosophical language. Hall and Ames demonstrate:

> The concern that Confucius has for the relational self and the communication that effects it is a major theme throughout the *Analects*. The identification and articulation of interests and importances is the basis for person building and the inclusion of others in one's filed of selves. The authoritative person inherits the values and significance of his culture and contributes to it in a process of symbolic exchange dominated by the medium of language. This language is performative in the sense that, for the authoritative person, saying requires the enactment of what is said in order to be true.[61]

Thus, *ren* is the basis of human relations in order to understand the meaning of the self in the *Analects*. The self can be fulfilled when he or she

---

59. *Analects*, 202, book 17:6.

60. I have been trying to find this concept of relational-self in other academic areas like theology and psychology. Stanley Grenz uses this term "relational self" in his book *The Social God and the Relational Self*, in order to depict the theological meaning of trinity and humanity. He had tried to find the connection between the divine relationality and the relational human self in this book. On the other hand, I found this term, the "relational self," through the study of religious psychology. And James W. Jones explains a psychological understanding of relational-self in his article "Relational Self: Contemporary Psychoanalysis Reconsiders Religion." He writes that several post-Freudian and post-Jungian psychologists have been trying to overcome the subject-object psychoanalysis which focuses on the individuality; instead, they began to adopt a relational model of the self in order to propose an interpersonal and interactional model of personality.

61. Hall and Ames, *Thinking through Confucius*, 123.

acknowledges their relatedness through *ren*. Namely, Confucian anthropology is based on the thought that humans are basically inclined toward *ren* and that the kernel of human relation is human-heartedness toward others. Therefore, the gist of anthropology in the *Analects* is the fulfillment of humanity, which is accomplished by the Way (*tao*) of self-transformation toward human heartedness (*ren*) based upon the notion of the relatedness of humanity.

All in all, Kongzi, as the transmitter of the traditions of the legendary Sage Kings in ancient China, follows the Way of Heaven and humanity as he practices Virtue. This is also the way to become an exemplary person (*junzi*) who actualizes *ren* in his or her daily life. *Ren* is, thus, the self-realization of human relatedness, that is, otherness. The human being fulfills his or her humanity through the consistent practice of *ren*. This is the foundation of humanness. In the next section, I will explore more about the inter-human relation in the *Analects*, as a foundation of the ethics of otherness.

Chapter 6

Humanness (*Ren*) and Others

AS I DISCUSSED ABOVE, one of the common misunderstandings of Confucianism is that it does not have the full sense of the autonomous self, which comes from the communitarian view of Confucianism as it concentrates on human relatedness. Confucianism, however, holds a clear implication of selfhood, which comes from its conception of humanness within *ren*. Also, this conception of *ren* is the foundation of human relatedness, which can be called intersubjectivity or the relational self. In this chapter, I will explore how Kongzi understands the self and others, and how he constantly argues that *ren* is the basis of humanness not only for individuals but also for others in terms of his conceptualization of learning (*xui*), ritual propriety (*li*), and understanding of others (*shu*).

Ren, Self-Cultivation, and *Xui* (Learning)

Ren and self-cultivation are the crux of the comprehension of the self in Confucianism. In particular, moral self-cultivation is the main key of the conception of the self in Kongzi.[1] Tu mentions the *Analects*, book 6:28, with his own translation, in order to show this tenet, "in order to establish oneself, one should try to establish others; in order to enlarge oneself, one should try to enlarge others."[2] Slingerland's translation of this passage illus-

---

1. Tu, "The Value of the Human in Classical Confucian Thought," in *Confucian Thought*, 67–80. See also Tu, "Embodying the Universe: A Note on Confucian Self-Realization," in Ames et al., *Self as Person*, 177–86.

2. Tu, "Value of the Human," 68. This passage, *Analects*, book 6:28, is the same as book 6:30 in the later translation of Ames, Lau, and Singerland.

trates this feature, with more details: "Desiring to take his stand, one who is Good helps others to take their stand; wanting to realize himself, he helps others to realize themselves."[3] One of Kongzi's disciples, Master Zeng says:

> Every day I examine myself on three counts: in my dealings with others, have I in any way failed to be dutiful? In my interactions with friends and associates, have I in any way failed to be trustworthy? Finally, have I in any way failed to repeatedly put into what I teach?[4]

Tu comments on this passage:

> This attempt to inform one's moral self-development by constantly probing one's inner self is neither a narcissistic search for private truth nor an individualistic claim for isolated experience. Rather, it is a form of self-cultivation which is simultaneously also a communal act of harmonizing human relationships.[5]

When Zilu asked about the way of *junzi*, Kongzi taught that "he (*junzi*) cultivates himself in order to achieve respectfulness," "to bring peace to others," and "to bring peace to all people."[6] Thus, *cultivating-self* in *humanness* (*ren*) creates a foundation for a person to stand as himself or herself, as Kongzi describes himself, "at thirty, I took my place in society," which means that Kongzi stands in his place among others.[7] This is also Kongzi's idea of *keji fuli*, restraint of oneself and return to propriety and goodness.[8]

Learning (*xue*) is the main "process of the training of the self" that makes the self stand *in and for* the world and the culture.[9] Tu demonstrates, "Learning is a way to be human and not simply a program of making oneself empirically knowledgeable. The whole process seeks to enrich the self, to enhance its strength and to refine its wisdom so that one can be considerate to others and honest with oneself."[10] With this implication, learning is

---

Chan's translation is similar to Tu's as, "a man of humanity, wishing to establish his own character, also establishes the character of others, and wishing to be prominent himself, also help others to be prominent" (Chan, *Source Book in Chinese Philosophy*, 31).

3. *Analects*, 63, book 6:30.
4. Ibid., 2, book 1:4.
5. Tu, "Value of the Human," 67.
6. *Analects*, 171, book 14:42.
7. Ibid., 9, book 2:4.
8. Ibid., 125, book 12:1.
9. Tu, "Value of the Human," 68.
10. Ibid.

moral self-cultivation. Gradually, people can build their moral characters for themselves in order to be responsive to common values and culture with others in their own society.[11] The first consideration of learning in Kongzi is the attitude of *love learning*. Kongzi says, "In any village of ten households there are surely those who are as dutiful or trustworthy as I am, but there is no one who matches my love for learning."[12] Love learning is the prerequisite not only for cultivating self, but also for following Goodness (*ren*). Kongzi creates an interesting parable to interpret this point of love learning as he notes, "I have yet to meet a man who loves Virtue as much as he loves female beauty."[13] If someone does love learning as he or she pursues fleshly pleasure or even material needs, this is the right way to cultivate self as simply as they can.

In particular, Kongzi explains learning as the process of self-cultivation as he teaches that people should concentrate themselves on the Way with the method of self-cultivation through the learning of Virtue. As if we are appreciating and mastering an art, or as if we are filing up a mountain, self-cultivation is an ongoing process of humanity to learn and fulfill Virtue. Kongzi says to "set your heart upon the Way, rely upon Virtue, lean upon Goodness, and explore widely in your cultivation of the arts."[14] He illustrates self-cultivation further:

> [The task of self-cultivation] might be compared to the task of building up a mountain: if I stop even one basketful of earth short of completion, then I have stopped completely. It might also be compared to the task of leveling ground: even if I have only dumped a single basketful of earth, at least I am moving forward.[15]

Thus, the right method to cultivate self is the learning of Virtue. The way of learning in the *Analects* is not a process of achieving knowledge, but it is the Way to acknowledge the attitude of life as following Virtue. The attitude of life comes from the understanding of the Way and it makes people love learning as I discussed above. The love of learning is metaphorically a process of cutting, polishing, carving, and grinding of the virtues of the self.[16] Hence, Kongzi teaches, "Learn as if you will never catch up, and as if

11. Ibid.
12. *Analects*, 51, book 5:28.
13. Ibid., 92, book 9:18. Also see book 15:13.
14. Ibid., 65, book 7:6.
15. Ibid., 93, book 9:19.
16. Ibid., 6–7, book 1:15.

Humanness (Ren) and Others

you feared losing what you have already attained."[17] Moreover, the practice of Virtue is the best way to "learning," in that Virtue cannot be gleaned by reading books, but in the action of virtue even if it is a very small thing in life. Namely, all "learning" comes from the real action of humanity toward *ren*. Kongzi demonstrates:

> A young person should be filial when at home and respectful of his elders when in public. Conscientious and trustworthy, he should display a general care for the masses but feel a particular affection for those who are Good. If he has any strength left over after manifesting these virtues in practice, let him devote it to learning the cultural arts (*wen*).[18]

Then, Kongzi insists that the practice of Virtue is the real "learning" even if someone does not engage in an official educational program.[19] Kongzi illustrates this as he explains his worry:

> That I fail to cultivate Virtue, that I fail to inquire more deeply into that I which I have learned, that upon hearing what is right I remain unable to move myself to do it, and that I prove unable to reform when I have done something wrong—such potential failings are a source of constant worry to me.[20]

His concern is not the matter of whether or not he is recognized by others, but rather his lack of ability to practice Virtue, since people "[do] not praise a thoroughbred horse for its physical strength, but rather for its character (*de*)."[21] Thus, the Way of learning of Virtue is based on self-cultivation, and only the cultivated-self can become the virtuoso as he or she shows themselves as the followers of *ren*.

Kongzi articulates his idea of learning as he values thinking, and participating in learning, as saying, "If you learn without thinking about what you have learned, you will be lost. If you think without learning, however, you will fall into danger."[22] Again, the balance of learning and thinking is critical for students because learning is not a simple process of gathering knowledge, but it is the self-cultivating process to practice Virtue. More-

---

17. Ibid., 83, book 8:17.
18. Ibid., 3, book 1:6.
19. Ibid., book 1:7.
20. Ibid., 64, book 7:2.
21. Ibid., 166–67, book 14:30 and 33.
22. Ibid., 13, book 2:15.

over, learning is an active participation in what students were taught, as Kongzi notes: "Learn as if you will never catch up, and as if you feared losing what you have already attained."[23] Unless students keep thinking and participating actively in *ren* and Virtue, they cannot cultivate themselves in order to be the students of the Way. Kongzi teaches this attitude of learning as he emphasizes "both keeping past teachings alive and understanding the present."[24]

For instance, Kongzi epitomizes Yan Hui as the real person who loves learning and practicing Virtue. When Duke Ai asked, "Who among your disciples might be said to love learning?" Kongzi answered, "There was one named Yan Hui who loved learning. He never misdirected his anger and never made the same mistake twice."[25] Again, Kongzi exemplified Yan Hui as a good learner: "I observed his private behavior, I see that it is in fact worthy to serve as an illustration of what I have taught."[26] "Ah, Yan Hui! For three months at a time his heart did not stray from Goodness (*ren*)."[27] "One with whom I could discourse without his growing weary—was this not Yan Hui?"[28] "I watched his advance, and never once saw him stop."[29] "Yan Hui is of no help to me—he is pleased with everything that I say."[30] These examples demonstrate Yan Hui's mindfulness, steadfastness, and joyfulness for learning, as a good illustration of thinking and participation. These show us how thinking and participation works into the process of learning in ways that Yan Hui kept his way to reflect himself as a follower of what he learned and how he followed the Way of *ren*. With this implication, the explanation of learning by Zixia, one of Kongzi's disciples, is conclusive in significance for learning, in that Zixia claims, "Learning broadly and firmly retaining what one has learned, being incisive in one's questioning and able to reflect upon what is near at hand—Goodness is to be found in this."[31] Thus, self-cultivation through the ongoing process of learning illustrates the embodiment of the self in the *Analects*, not because it guarantees more

23. Ibid., 83, book 8:17.
24. Ibid., 11, book 2:11.
25. Ibid., 53, book 6:3.
26. Ibid., 11, book 2:9.
27. Ibid., 55, book 6:7 (parenthesis is mine).
28. Ibid., 93, book 9:20.
29. Ibid., 94, book 9:21.
30. Ibid., 112, book 11:4.
31. Ibid., 223, book 19:6.

individual benefits for people, but because it opens and finalizes the Way of *ren*. That is also the Way of *junzi*, as "the gentleman learns in order to reach the end of his Way."[32]

Ren and *Li* (Ritual Propriety)

The comprehension of *li* (ritual propriety) is a prerequisite to explore otherness in Confucianism. *Li* is the concrete actualization of *ren* as it values the other and human relation as humanity participates in rituals. Tu values Kongzi's phrase, "at seventy, I could follow my heart's desires without overstepping the bounds of propriety,"[33] in order to deal with the "creative tension between *jen* (*ren*) and *li*."[34] Tu explains that *ren* and self-cultivation are actualized by ritual propriety (*li*), as he demonstrates:

> Confucius claimed that at seventy he could follow his heart's desires, and yet every act performed by him was in line with *li*. This does not mean that he had become a virtuoso of *li*. It suggests, instead, that he was able to bridge the seemingly unbridgeable gap between "what is" and "what ought to be." He was so versed in self-cultivation that he could operate in a specific social situation with an artistic maturity. In fact, Confucius used the image of music to describe type of perfect harmony between ones' inwardness and outer manifestation.[35]

Tu argues that *ren* is not only the primary tenet of the inwardness of humanity. Namely, *ren* is not an obtained-quality from the outside, but it is the self-cultivating, self-fulfilling, and self-reviving process of humanity. In order to externalize *ren* in humanity, *li* manifests *ren* in the social context of human being.[36] Tu recapitulates that "*jen* (*ren*), as a Confucian ideal, is universalistic rather than particularistic, but in the real process through which *jen* (*ren*) is concretely actualized, particular considerations in the

---

32. Ibid., 223, book 19:7.
33. Ibid., 9, book 2:4.
34. Tu, *Humanity and Self-Cultivation*, 14 (parenthesis is mine).
35. Ibid. In the sense of music, Tu cited the *Analects*, book 3:3, in his book *Humanity and Self-cultivation*, 7. In this passage, Kongzi said, "A man who is not Good—what has he to do with ritual? A man who is not Good—what has he to do with music?"
36. Ibid., 9–10.

realm of *li* do exist."³⁷ This is the way of Kongzi that accomplishes his ideal of self-cultivation in the social context.³⁸

Likewise, Herbert Fingarette explains the relation between *ren* and *li* as he articulates that humanity does not exist as an individual self; rather, each person is a participant in a ceremonial performance of the communal ritual in order to fulfill humanity.³⁹ *Ren* is not only the main theme of the ritual, but also the source of it. While humans are joining in a ritual, they acknowledge and recognize themselves as communal beings through their ceremonial relations. Fingarette emphasizes that

> Confucius does not see the individual as an ultimate atom nor society on the analogy of animal or mechanism, nor does he see society as a proving around for immortal souls or a contractual or utilitarian arrangement designed to maximize individual pleasure. He does not talk in the Analects of society and the individual. . . . To become civilized is to establish relationships that are not merely physical, biological or instinctive; it is to establish *human* relationships, relationship of an essentially symbolic kind, defined by tradition and convention and rooted in respect and obligation.⁴⁰

Correspondingly, he demonstrates that *ren* is "the perfect giving of oneself to the *human* way" in that humans can treat others as equal as they can through *li*, the actualization of *ren*.⁴¹ *Ren* reveals its own power while it performs the communal ritual. It radiates the performance, not because it has acted overtly, but because it has stressed the actual course of the communal ritual. The power of *ren* makes people radiate for themselves because it has the authority of continual participation in rituals. Fingarette illustrates the power of *ren*:

> This power is to be essentially *human* power; that is, it is a power of human beings (when they *are* truly human) and it is directed *toward* human beings and influences them. The Chinese of Confucius has not clear distinction between properties, qualities, definitions or essences. But we can say that *jen* is often directly associated with a *person* and suggested to be a possession of the person.⁴²

---

37. Ibid., 11–12 (parenthesis is mine).
38. Ibid., 12–13.
39. Fingarette, *Confucius*, ch. 5.
40. Ibid., 77 (italics original).
41. Ibid., 53–54, 56 (italics original).
42. Ibid., 54–55 (italics original). *Jen* is same with *ren*.

Thus, *ren* and *li* inspire human being to realize humanness, that is, the valuation of human relatedness.

Li does not mean a simple practice of rituals, but it is the holistic approach to others with respect through participation in it. Since *ren* is the manifestation of human relation, *li* is the practical participation into human relation not only with ritual in itself but also with the practical service for each human relation. For instance, in Kongzi, filial piety (*xiao*) and respect for elders (*ti*) are not only the constitution and the root of *ren*,[43] but they are also the genuine way to participate in politics.[44] Then, he argues that filial piety is not a simple sacrifice for parents, but it is the lifelong obedience and respect to them with ritual propriety (*li*). When Meng asked about filial piety, Kongzi answered first, "Do not disobey," and then, "When your parents are alive, serve them in accordance with the rites; when they pass away, bury them in accordance with the rites and sacrifice to them in accordance with the rites."[45] In addition, Kongzi says, "Nowadays 'filial' means simply being able to provide one's parents with nourishment. But even dogs and horses are provided with nourishment. If you are not respectful, wherein lies the difference?"[46] With the sense of *li*, filial piety is not a simple obedience to parents, but the respect to them, as an example of the way of *ren*. Furthermore, *li* is the foundation of the ruling authority of the sage kings to their people within a more broad human relation. In our common sense, *li* is a virtue which people have to show to their rulers, yet, in the *Analects*, ritual is the source that "a lord should employ his ministers," then, the loyalty and dutifulness of the ministers will be followed spontaneously for their rulers.[47] Kongzi demonstrates the principle of governing people with *li* and *ren*:

> If your wisdom reaches it, but your Goodness (*ren*) cannot protect it, then even though you may have attained it, you are sure to eventually lose it. If your wisdom reaches it, and your Goodness is able to protect it, but you cannot manifest it with dignity, then the common people will not be respectful. If your wisdom reaches it, your Goodness is able to protect it, and you can manifest it with

---

43. *Analects*, 1, book 1:2.
44. Ibid., 15, book 2:21.
45. Ibid., 9, book 2:5.
46. Ibid., 10, book 2:7.
47. Ibid., 25, book 3:19.

dignity, but you do not use ritual (*li*) to put it into motion, it will never truly excellent.⁴⁸

Kongzi, thus, values *li* as the praxis of *ren* in human relation, not because it is an artificial gesture of people to build a sound relationship, but because it is the way to have truthful humanness; as Kongzi recapitulates, "Let the lord be a true lord, the ministers true ministers, the fathers true fathers, and the sons true sons."⁴⁹

In this implication, *li* is actualized by harmony, and vice versa. Harmony does not simply mean to agree on almost everything with others,⁵⁰ but it is attentive to others with *li*, as it actualizes the Way of *ren* through *li*. Master You, a disciple of Kongzi, elaborates the feature of harmony:

> When it comes to the practice of ritual, it is harmonious ease (*he*) that is to be valued. It is precisely such harmony that makes the Way of the Former Kings so beautiful. If you merely stick rigidly to ritual in all matters, great and small, there will remain that which you cannot accomplish. Yet if you know enough to value harmonious ease but try to attain it without being regulated by the rites, this will not work either.⁵¹

Ritual propriety (*li*) demonstrates the harmonious way. Again, *junzi* always try to harmonize himself or herself with others according to *li*, but he or she does not try to uniformatize themselves with others. Namely, *junzi* does not try to equalize himself or herself to others; rather, they values the differences among people, and then, makes harmony in their relationships.⁵² This is what the golden rule says, "Do not impose upon others what you yourself do not desire."⁵³ Kongzi illustrates this aspect with more details: "When in public, comport yourself as if you were receiving an important guest, and in your management of the common people, behave as if you were overseeing a great sacrifice."⁵⁴ *Junzi* is broadminded, but not partial because of this harmonious life style.⁵⁵ Kongzi shows another example of

---

48. Ibid., 187, book 15:33 (parenthesis is mine).
49. Ibid., 130, book 12:11.
50. Ibid., 149, book 13:23.
51. Ibid., 5, book 1:12 (parenthesis by translator).
52. Ibid., 149, book 13:23.
53. Ibid., 126, book 12:2.
54. Ibid.
55. Ibid., 12, book 2:14.

harmony as he valued music with poetry and ritual propriety (*li*). Kongzi says, "Find inspiration in the *Odes*, take your place through ritual, and achieve perfection with music,"[56] and more:

> What can be now about music is this: when it first begins, it resounds with a confusing variety of notes, but as it unfolds, these notes are reconciled by means of harmony, brought into tension by means of counterpoint, and finally woven together into a seamless whole. It is in the way that music reaches its perfection.[57]

Stephen C. Angle articulates that harmony is fruitful, novel and creative, as he notes, "Harmony can be said to be 'creative' in two senses. First, it is fruitful, in terms of what follows after this moment. Harmony leads to productive and constructive outcomes. Second, harmony can be novel. With imagination, we can see and achieve new points of balance."[58] As we read the valuation of the musician, this novelty and fruitfulness comes from consistent participation in *li* in order to reach the perfection of harmony.

Li should not be extravagant nor boastful because it comes from the respect for others and humility of the self; instead, it has to be humble and tentative for others. For instance, when Kongzi served the royal rituals in the Great Ancestral Temple, he asked everything what he had to do. At that time, someone criticized that Kongzi did not know the rituals because of this attitude; then, Kongzi replied, "This asking is, in fact, part of ritual."[59] This anecdote shows Kongzi's politeness, carefulness, and humility when he serves the rituals. In the other sense, Kongzi values ritual itself more than any other humanistic approaches to ritual. Once Zigong tried to practice a sacrifice without lamb, and Kongzi said, "Zigong! You regret the loss of lamb, whereas I regret the loss of the rite."[60] Sincerity and consistency in ritual is more important than any artificial interpretation of ritual. Another example occurred when Zai Wo asked about the three-year mourning period, arguing, "Surely one year is long enough. If the gentleman refrains from practicing ritual for three years, the rites will surely fall into ruin; if he refrains from music for three years, this will be surely disastrous for music." Kongzi answered, "Do it as you wish if you feel comfortable."[61] Yet,

56. Ibid., 80, book 8:8.
57. Ibid., 27, book 3:23.
58. Angle, *Sagehood*, 65.
59. *Analects*, 23, book 3:15.
60. Ibid., 24, book 3:17.
61. Ibid., 209–10, book 17:21.

Kongzi explained why he wanted to observe a three-year mourning period: "A child is completely dependent upon the care of his parents for the first three years of his life—this is why the three-year mourning period is the common practice throughout the world. Did Zai Wo not receive three years of care from his parents?" Kongzi finally rebuked Zai Wo as lacking of *ren*.[62] In this sense, *li* reveals our basic attitude to others whether or not we are sincere, humble, consistent, and careful of them. Thus, *li* actualizes *ren* through our participation in rituals.

Ren and *Shu* (Understanding of Others)

The conception of *shu* (understanding of others) is another critical foundation of understanding human relatedness and otherness in the *Analects*. Since the externalization of *ren* is *li*, the conception of *shu* is the internalization of *ren* for the harmonious human relation, which is the Golden rule in human relation. Kongzi mentioned the Golden rule directly twice in the *Analects* in the passage in book 12:2 and 15:24, when his disciples, Zhonggong and Zigong asked about ren. In particular, when Zigong asked, "Is there one word that can serve as a guide for ones entire life?" Kongzi answered, "Is it not 'understanding' (*shu*)? Do not impose upon others what you yourself do not desire."[63] Kongzi explains *shu* with more details in *Book of Mean*:

> The Way is not far from man. When a man pursues the Way and yet remains away from man, his course cannot be considered the Way. The *Book of Odes* says, "in hewing an axe handle, in hewing an axe handle, the pattern is not far off." If we take an axe handle to hew another axe handle and look askance from the one to the other, we may still think the pattern is far away. Therefore the superior man (*junzi*) governs men as men, in accordance with human nature, and as soon as they change [what is wrong], he stops. Conscientiousness (*chung*) and altruism (*shu*) are not far from the Way. What you do not wish other to do to you, do not do to them.[64]

There is another example to demonstrate this point in the conversation between Kongzi and Zigong:

62. Ibid.
63. Ibid., 183, book 15:24. See also book 5:12.
64. Chan, ed., *Source Book in Chinese Philosophy*, 100–101.

Humanness (Ren) and Others

Zigong said, "If there were one able to broadly extend his benevolence to the common people and bring succor to the multitudes, what would make of him? Could such a person be called Good?"

The Master said, "Why stop at Good? Such a person should surely be called a sage! Even someone like Yao or Shun would find such a task daunting. Desiring to take his stand, one who is Good helps others to take their stand; wanting to realize himself, he helps others to realize themselves. Being able to take what is near at hand as an analogy could be called the method of Goodness."[65]

The Way, thus, does not come from outside of humanity, but it is found in the middle of human relation, that is, in understanding of others (*shu*).

Although *shu* is translated with various meanings, i.e., altruism (Chan), reciprocity (Tu and de Bary),[66] understanding (Slingerland), empathy (Brooks),[67] and deference (Hall and Ames),[68] it is the one thread of Kongzi, which is the foundation of human relation.[69] Among these features of *shu*, altruism and reciprocity cannot fully grasp the concept of *shu* because Confucian thoughts are based on human relatedness rather than ontological reciprocity. Human relatedness occurs prior to the individual notion of altruism or communal reciprocity. Instead, human relatedness values alterity more than reciprocity because of the uniqueness and priority of otherness in human relation. Thus, understanding and deference are the concrete grounds of human relations in the *Analects*. In particular, the idea of deference demonstrates the one thread of Kongzi because *shu* is *within and beyond* the reciprocal understanding of human relation. Hall and Ames argue that

> *Shu* is not simply taking oneself as the model and projecting it onto other; rather, it is first clarifying oneself on terms of other, and then either in personal relations. *Shu*, then, is both the act of deferring and the demand for deference. . . .

---

65. *Analects*, 63, book 6:30.
66. Tu, *Centrality and Commonality*; Tu, *Confucian Thought*; and De Bary, *Sources of East Asian Tradition*, 1:39.
67. Brooks and Taeko, trans., *Original Analects*, 137.
68. Hall and Ames, *Thinking through Confucius*, 285–96.
69. I mentioned the *Analects*, book 4:15 and book 15:3 in order to discuss this idea of one thread of Kongzi. In particular, book 4:15 claimed the one thread is dutifulness (*zhong*) and understanding (*shu*) as Master Zeng, one of Kongzi's disciples, explained it. *Zhong* is the same word as *chung*.

Part III: Confucius (Kongzi) and the Analects

> In asserting that *shu* is to be understood in terms of giving and receiving deference, we are making a rather far-reaching claim.... One of the most significant implications of our discussion of *shu* as deference is that the activity of thinking itself must be understood in terms of *shu*.[70]

Based on this argument, Hall and Ames compare their interpretation of *shu* with Derrida's concept of *différance*. As *différance* plays its illustration of difference with or against both the passive and active dimension in time and space with the linguistic nuances of differing and deferring, the Confucian concept of difference includes both senses of the acts of differing as being distinct and the notion of deferring as postponing. This postponement is not established by the idea of reference, but through deference, that is, yielding.[71] Therefore,

> the language of deference is the language of *shu*. ... The recognition of excellence in tradition or in interpersonal relations occasions a yielding to that excellence which, when communicated appropriately, serves as a model to which other will also yield. This yielding begins with "listening." Confucius first "listens" to the excellences of tradition and of present praxis and through this deferential act thereby attunes himself. Only in so doing does he constitute himself as a model calling forth deference from others.[72]

Shu, as deference, thus, depends on both similarity and difference among people and their activities, or circumstances that create the harmonies in the personal, interpersonal, and social relation.[73]

Kongzi describes various approaches to *shu*. Even if a person does not achieve fame or a name among others, he or she does not need to worry, but *junzi* has to think of others first. Nor does he or she have to criticize others because *junzi* does not have enough time to do this at all. Rather, *junzi* evaluates himself or herself whether or not they keep *shu* in their mind. Kongzi teaches, "Do not be concerned about whether or not others know you; be concerned about whether or not you know others."[74] When Zigong criticized others, Kongzi rebuked him, saying, "What a worthy man that

---

70. *Thinking through Confucius*, 289–90.
71. Ibid., 292–93.
72. Ibid., 295–96. Also see, *Analects*, book 2:4 and book 12:2.
73. Ibid., 296.
74. *Analects*, 7, book 1:16.

Humanness (Ren) and Others

Zigong must be! As for me, I hardly have the time for this."[75] Kongzi said again, "Do not worry that you are not recognized by others; worry rather that you yourself lack ability."[76] This is a passive action of *shu* for *junzi*; *shu* also formulates an active action in being *junzi* with trustworthiness and supportiveness for others. Kongzi claims, "Not anticipating betrayal, nor expecting untrustworthiness, yet still being the first to perceive it—this is a worthy person indeed."[77] With trusting, *junzi* does not only escape any possibility of betrayal of others, but he or she also supports and cares for others in elevating their Goodness (*ren*). Kongzi instructs that "a gentleman helps others to realize their good qualities, rather than their bad,"[78] and this is the way that "the gentleman acquires friends by means of cultural refinement, and then relies upon his friends for support in becoming Good."[79] As I mentioned above, when Fan Chi asked about *ren*, Kongzi answered, "Care for others," and more importantly, "Know others."[80] Caring and knowing others in terms of *shu* makes people accurate and impartial in their relationships, i.e., "only one who is Good is able to truly love others or despise others."[81] Thus, *shu* is another foundation of human relatedness, in that *shu* values and understands others by acting in deference, i.e., yielding, trusting, caring, and supporting.

Overall, Kongzi has a clear understanding of the self and intersubjectivity in the *Analects*. Kongzi cultivates himself through a lifetime learning process as he himself practices *ren*. Thus, the notion of the self is acquired by this cultivating process of the self in the Confucian tradition. This self-cultivation is based on human relatedness as Kongzi constantly demonstrates that *ren* is the basis of humanness not only for the self but also for others through ritual propriety (*li*), and understanding of others (*shu*). *Li* is the externalization of *ren*; whereas, *shu* is the internal foundation of *ren* within deference of the self and understanding others. In the next chapter, I will explore the ethical features of *ren* in the *Analects*, as I delve into the significance of Virtue, *wu-wei* (effortless action), and the sense of community in Kongzi.

75. Ibid., 165, book 14:29.
76. Ibid., 166, book 14:30.
77. Ibid, book 14:31.
78. Ibid., 133, book 12:16.
79. Ibid., 137, book 12:24.
80. Ibid., 136, book 12:22.
81. Ibid., 30, book 4:3.

Chapter 7

Ren and Ethics

THERE ARE THREE THEMES in this chapter: why *ren* becomes the foundation of Confucian morality, what Kongzi teaches about *ren* in terms of ethics, and how Confucian ethics values community and society. *Ren* is not a simple understanding of humanness, but a driving force of human morality. Kongzi teaches morality based on his concept of Virtue (*de*). The primary goal of Kongzi is to build an ideal society as he practiced *ren*. Based on these ideas, I will explore the main ethical features in the *Analects* in terms of morality and Virtue, Confucian moral actions with the concepts of timeliness and effortlessness, and Kongzi's ideas and endeavors for building a fiduciary community.

Ren, Tao, and Ethics

Zehua Liu and Quan Ge argued the kernel of ethics in classical Confucianism as they compared the thought of humanity and democracy between Confucianism and the Euro-American theory. Both writers were trying to criticize that Confucianism is not able to fit into the modern democratic political system since its ethical principles are based on "human social life," related to "a group of norms of a patrarchical (patriarchal) society" rather than "universality" in terms of individual freedom and responsibility which is the gist of social development.[1] Although they read Confucianism with a different prism ironically, their understanding of Confucian ethics is so

---

1. Liu and Quan Ge, "On the 'Human' in Confucianism," 318. I think that there is a typo here. In the original copy, the word patrarchial appeared, but the real word is "patriarchal."

comprehensive that their analysis can explain the kernel of Confucian ethics, related to their thoughts of modernity:

> First and foremost, the human position as a subject, its subjectivity, is built on the basis of the assumption that the human being is the active agent that not only receives what nature provides but also always tries to change and control the world. Similarly, the evolution of civilization is also dependent upon and parallel to human action's changing the objective world. Confucianism shows us a different picture of humanity; here, ethics is held to be the essence of the human, which supersedes and trivializes every other possibility. From the Confucian point of view, the significance and meaning of human existence lies in humans' recognition and cultivation of their own ethical nature.[2]

Their criticism of the Confucian tradition is overarching to our understanding of modern humanity because it presents an understanding of the humanity of Confucianism as limited and restricted, since its communitarian social understanding is considered as patriarchal and hierarchal. However, it is not legitimate to criticize Confucian ethics as its own limitedness and restriction. Rather, their interpretation of Confucian ethics explains an important aspect of ethics, in that ethics is not only the issue of individual agency, but it also is the issue of human-relatedness to fulfill humanity. The elucidation of humanness is the difference between Confucian ethics and the Euro-American tradition of ethics. With this different implication of ethics between both traditions, there are two main ethical arguments in the *Analects*: the issue of the right and the good, and the comprehension of Virtue.

Before we move into these ethical arguments of Confucian ethics, it is necessary to look at the ethical construal of the Way in order to analyze these issues. The social relation is based on the practice of *li* and *shu* through lifelong dedication to learning for the process of self-cultivation. This is, in a sense, an individual obligation for others; in another sense, this is an ethical participation into the harmonious community. The sense of obligation does not imply the personal duty for others, but it is the obedience and resoluteness to "complete *ren*" in order to fulfill humanness.[3] The significance of participation into the harmonious community is also the process to complete *ren* as a person, in particular, as a *junzi*, cultivating

---

2. Ibid., 318–19.
3. See *Analects*, book 1:3, 4:5, 4:8.

himself or herself through participating in *li*, and maintaining *shu*. This process of completion of *ren* is the Way in Kongzi. Ivanhoe articulates Kongzi's perspective of the Way and ethics as such:

> The moral life is the life lived cultivating oneself for participation in this grand and harmonious community. However, one's commitment is not simply a matter of enlightened self-interest; playing one's part in the great Way affords one the unique opportunity of fulfilling one's destiny as a human being. The relationships one enters into as a member of such a society are not regarded as restrictive; they are seen as profoundly fulfilling. They give one the opportunity to develop oneself and work as part of a larger social whole that not only affords one unique opportunities for direct personal fulfillment but also expresses a particular conception of what it is to be a human being.[4]

Thus, the Way constantly motivates people to implement humanness through ritual propriety (*li*) and deference to others (*shu*). Also, ethics in Kongzi is not a simple recognition of a personal goodness, but it is the obedience toward the Way of *ren*.

The issue of the wrong and the good is another critical matter in Confucian ethics. The Euro-American thinkers argue that Confucian ethics does not have a patent perception of the right and the wrong. Namely, Confucian ethics does not have a universal norm of right and wrong, but it is unpredictable according to personal situations. Mozi, a contemporary thinker of Kongzi, made a severe criticism of this issue. He said that Kongzi was a hypocrite because the ethical practice of Kongzi focused only on funeral rituals that led people to waste wealth and energy. Kongzi lacked the idea of universal all-embracing love, but he made people feel the burden, and then become lethargic and even lazy because of the ceaseless practice of rituals.[5] The legalists, i.e., Hanfeizi, during the Warring States Period, also criticized Kongzi, as arguing that Confucian ethics does not have a sense of law and social justice, since a nation has to be built on a foundation of strong law instead of governing by *li*.[6] These criticisms are caused by Kongzi's practice of *li*, and a timely reaction of circumstances and his interpretation of it in human relation. For instance, the conversation between

---

4. Ivanhoe, *Ethics in the Confucian Tradition*, 3–4.
5. Fung, *Short History of Chinese Philosophy*, 52–55. See also *Mengzi*, 73–74, book 3A5.
6. Ibid., ch. 14.

the Duke of *She* and Kongzi provides an example of a serious argument in terms of the issue of the right:

> The Duke of She said to Confucius, "Among my people there is one we call 'Upright Gong.' When his father stole a sheep, he reported him to the authorities."
>
> Confucius replied, "Among my people, those who we considered 'upright' are different from this: fathers cover up for their sons, and sons cover up for their fathers. 'Uprightness' is to be found in this."[7]

The uprightness in this passage brings an argument of Confucian ethics. Cline, paradoxically, argues that this passage shows another basic feature of Confucian ethics. To begin with,

> good ends must be achieved in accordance with the Way or he will not abide them, and bad ends must be avoided in accordance with the Way or he will not despise them. The Way is not just about achieving good ends; it is also about doing the right thing, and Kongzi refuses to celebrate good ends that were achieved in the wrong way.[8]

Cline argues more that

> Kongzi clearly thinks that following the Way is sometimes to the detriment of achieving a good outcome in the short term, and he maintains that one should follow the Way even when it will result in such losses. On this view, following the Way means doing the right thing and going about things in the right way. One takes a series of steps that build upon and reinforce on another, keeping the long term in mind and believing that one is doing the right thing according to Heaven's plan. Only this will allow one to achieve and maintain the true aim.[9]

Based on this argument, Cline demonstrates that ethics is not a matter of choice of one thing out of the right (obeying duties) nor the good (being virtuous). Instead, Confucian ethics follows in goodness according to what is right, and vice versa.[10]

---

7. *Analects*, 147, book 13:18. Compare with *Mengzi*, 180–81, book 7A35.
8. Cline, "The Way, the Right, and the Good," 114.
9. Ibid., 115.
10. Ibid., 121.

In addition, Cline explains three foci in this passage. First, Kongzi prioritizes the good which a person has to respond to this situation with the sense of the good for his or her father rather than doing the right according to the law.[11] Second, Kongzi more highly values the virtue of uprightness and the conduct out of this virtue than the rightness or its consequences of a certain action. Kongzi accounts responsibility according to filial piety as a more important basis of human relation.[12] Third, Kongzi follows the Way of Virtue in order to fulfill *ren*, instead he tries to create good outcome from a certain moral action.[13] Cline develops her interpretation of Confucian ethics based on the third approach of this passage, pointing out that to choose the good or the right is not an issue in Kongzi because when a person follows the Way, simultaneously, he or she can do what is right, that is, their lifelong commitment for the Way instead of a short-term good action. The ethical action in Kongzi, thus, is a long-term process to practice the Virtue of the Way that people are to follow "the right by obeying Heaven and following the Way," "to be good for us and others and leads toward the greater end of a harmonious society," and to recognize that "heaven has not other goal than promoting human flourishing."[14] Kongzi resonates the good and the right in his ethical thought as he emphasizes the following of the Virtue of the Way in order to fulfill humanity.

For instance, Kongzi illustrates the power of Virtue as the Pole Star that "it simply remains in its place and receives the homage of the myriad lesser stars."[15] With this implication, Kongzi emphasizes Virtue in politics: "If you guide them with Virtue, and keep them in line by means of ritual, the people will have a sense of shame and will rectify themselves."[16] This power of Virtue relies on effortless action (*wu-wei*) rather than coercive action. In particular, Kongzi exemplifies the Sage King, Shun, as the Pole Star: "Is Shun not an example of someone who ruled by means of *wu-wei*? What did he do? He made himself reverent and took his proper [ritual] position facing south, that is all."[17] The Sage King, Shun, seemed not to do anything for his people, but all nations and descendents admired him as

---

11. Ibid.
12. Ibid., 116–17.
13. Ibid., 118–19.
14. Ibid., 120.
15. *Analects*, 8, book 2:1.
16. Ibid, book 2:3.
17. Ibid., 175, book 15:5 (italics mine).

the Pole Star because of his power of Virtue and his appearance of the Way. Besides, when Zizhang asked about concrete conduct (*xing*) to follow the Way, Kongzi answered, "In your speech, be dutiful and trustworthy, and in your conduct be sincere and respectful. In this way, you will always get by in the world, even if you find yourself in some barbarian state."[18] Moreover, in this sense, Kongzi says, "The gentleman devotes his thoughts to attaining the Way, not to obtaining food. . . . The gentleman is concerned about the Way and not about poverty"[19] and "human beings can broaden the Way—it is not the Way that broadens human beings."[20] Finally, again, because "virtue is never solitary, it always has neighbors,"[21] people will spontaneously follow the Way and will act virtuously through effortless action.

Wu-wei (Effortless Action)

Kongzi does not try to formulate any ethical norms, nor even consider himself as an example of virtue. Rather, what he wants to do is to follow the Way and the Virtue of the Sage Kings as he obeys the *tien-ming* (heavenly mandate) as a transmitter. This is the paradoxical comprehension of moral action in Kongzi as he conceives the notion of effortless action (*wu-wei*). Kongzi did not want to become the sole Pole Star. Yet, he could be regarded as one of the Pole Stars just like the Sage Kings by his disciples and followers. Kongzi's personal autobiographical statement illustrates how he understands *wu-wei* such as that "at seventy, I could follow my heart's desires without overstepping the bounds of propriety."[22] Slingerland points out:

> Confucius places a great deal of emphasis upon the importance of "naturalness" in the moral life. One who has to force morally acceptable behavior is not, in the Confucius view, a truly moral person; a truly moral person dwells in morality as comfortably as in his own home, and the genuinely *ren* person can thus follow the spontaneous promptings of the heart/mind without overstepping the bounds.[23]

---

18. Ibid., 176, book 15:6.
19. Ibid., 187, book 15:32.
20. Ibid., 185, book 15:29.
21. Ibid., 37, book 4:25.
22. Ibid., 9, book 2:4.
23. Slingerland, *Effortless Action*, 70.

This ethical vision of Kongzi is the paradox of *wu-wei*. In common sense, rules and regulations are required for self-cultivation in itself in a common educational setting.[24] Namely, self-cultivation cannot be accomplished through a natural method like the example of Kongzi in the modern educational system. Kongzi, however, evaluates his way of moral action as an effortless action because learning is not a simple course of education, but the source of learning is to obey and to love the Way, Virtue, and *ren* which are the core of *wu-wei*.

Everyday practice of Virtue is the prerequisite in effortless action (*wu-wei*). Unless ethics transforms the awareness of everydayness, it will become a measurement to judge the moral inferiority of others or a tool of hypocrisy to boast of the moral superiority of an individual self. Ethics needs to be not only a mirror that reflects humanity's everydayness, but also a compass that guides humanity's routines to the right way of *ren*. Confucian ethics teaches us how our moral practices are related to Virtue, sincerity and harmony. Most of all, *junzi* does not practice Virtue with visual or artificial methods in order to show something outwardly, but he or she reveals the Way through their everydayness with effortless action. Kongzi uses excellent metaphors in order to explain effortless action, such as, "The Virtue of a gentleman is like a wind, and the Virtue of a petty person is like the grass—when the wind moves over the grass, the grass is sure to bend."[25] Zigong gives us another metaphor: "A gentleman's errors are like an eclipse of the sun or the moon: when he errs, everyone notices it, but when he makes amends, everyone looks up to him."[26] Kongzi actualizes this metaphor in his public and private life. For instance, when the Minister of Crime criticized Kongzi's partiality toward Duke Zhao, Kongzi accepted this criticism as he said, "How fortunate I am! If I happen to make a mistake, others are sure to inform me."[27] In addition, Kongzi practices Virtue, as he humbly

---

24. Ibid., 70–71. We can read another criticism of Kongzi's *wu-wei* by his contemporary Chinese philosophers like Laozi and Zhuangzi, the founders of Taoism. Slingerland demonstrates this criticism very clearly: "Both of these Daoist thinkers felt that the profound tension involved in training someone in traditional, artificial forms in order to allow them to act 'naturally' was a fatal flaw in Confucian thought and could only lead to spiritual hypocrisy" (*Effortless Action*, 75). Also see *Short History of Chinese Philosophy*, chs. 6 and 9.

25. *Analects*, 134, book 12:19.

26. Ibid., 228, book 19:21.

27. Ibid., 74–75, book 7:31.

always tries to understand "higher things."²⁸ Kongzi sometimes regrets that he does not reach the threefold achievement of *junzi*: "The Good do not worry, the wise are not confused, and the courageous do not fear."²⁹ He says more that "there is no one who is my equal when it comes to cultural refinement, but as for actually becoming a gentleman in practice, this is something that I have not yet been able to achieve."³⁰ Another good example of his humble attitude is in his practice of Virtue, as he states, "Whenever the Master was singing in a group and heard something that he liked, he inevitably asked to have it sung again, and only then would harmonize with it."³¹

In addition, the passage of book 2:12, "the gentleman (*junzi*) is not a vessel," demonstrates Kongzi's idea of *wu-wei* significantly.³² The literal meaning of vessel (*qi*) is the equipment that serves a particular function for rituals, and the metaphorical meaning of it is someone who is a specialist for a particular task. This feature is very important for the civilians, not only in this contemporary society, but also in Kongzi's era. This passage does not mean that Kongzi despises people's special tasks in their vocations;³³ instead, it demonstrates that *junzi* is working everything through Virtue, rather than their simple tasks. When Fan Chi asked about agriculture, Kongzi answered that he was not better in agriculture than farmers, but then Kongzi remarked about Fan Chi:

> What a common fellow (*xiaoren*—the opposite of *junzi*) that Fan Chi is! When a ruler loves ritual propriety, then none among his people will dare to be disrespectful. When a ruler loves rightness, then none among his people will dare not to obey. When a ruler loves trustworthiness, then none of his people will dare to not be honest. The mere existence of such a ruler would cause the common people throughout the world to bundle their children on their backs and seek him out. Of what use, then, is the study of agriculture?³⁴

---

28. Ibid., 164, book 14:23.
29. Ibid., 165, book 14:28.
30. Ibid., 75, book 7:33.
31. Ibid, book 7:32.
32. Ibid., 12, book 2:12.
33. See book 5:4. Kongzi evaluates one of his best pupils, Zigong, as a vessel, especially as the most important vessel for rituals (*hu-lian* vessel).
34. *Analects*, 140, book 13:4 (parenthesis is mine).

Again, this passage tells us not about the uselessness of agriculture, but about the action of *junzi* as the follower of the Way and the Virtue. In this sense, Kongzi emphasizes the accordance of the words of the people with their actions that "the gentleman is shamed to have his words exceed his actions,"[35] and the gentleman "first expresses his views, and then acts in accordance with them."[36] Also, he rebukes someone who speaks glibly and adorns himself or herself excessively, noting several times in the *Analects* that they don't have Goodness (*ren*).[37] Kongzi recapitulates nine things on which *junzi* has to focus:

> When looking, he focuses on seeing clearly; when listening, he focuses on being discerning; in his expression, he focuses on being amiable; in his demeanor, he focuses on being reverent; in his speech, he focuses on being dutiful; in his actions, he focuses on being respectful; when in doubt, he focuses on asking questions; when angry, he focuses on thinking about the potential negative consequences of his anger; and when seeing gain, he focuses upon what is right.[38]

Kongzi, thus, values the action of *junzi* based on the accordance with Virtue rather than any unnatural or artificial demeanors to achieve a particular purpose. This is the integrity and sincerity in *junzi*'s actions, which come from self-cultivation and the relation with others.

The most important tenet of *wu-wei* is "to bring peace to others" through the process of self-cultivation.[39] Most of all, again, *junzi* is to "feel at home in Goodness (*ren*)," since "without Goodness, one cannot remain constant in adversity and cannot enjoy enduring happiness."[40] Unless *junzi* feels at home in *ren*, he or she cannot truly love others, nor even despise others.[41] Easiness and peace in *ren*, thus, is the source of sincerity and impartiality in human relations. According to this notion, to "feel at home in

---

35. Ibid., 165, book 14:27.
36. Ibid., 12, book 2:13.
37. See book 1:3, 5:25, 15:27, 17:17. Also compare these with book 5:5, 11:25, 12:3, 16:4.
38. Ibid., 196, book 16:10.
39. Ibid., 171, book 14:42.
40. Ibid., 29, book 4:2.
41. Ibid., 30, book 4:3. The English translation of "to feel at home" and "to bring peace" comes from the same Chinese word, *an*. The etymology of this word is characterized by the picture of a woman staying in her home.

ren," *junzi* can bring peace for others through the moral action of *wu-wei*. In a long conversation with Zilu, Kongzi emphasizes this facet of *wu-wei*:

> Zilu asked about the gentleman.
> The Master said, "He cultivates himself in order to achieve respectfulness."
> "Is that all?"
> "He cultivates himself in order to bring peace to others."
> "Is that all?"
> "He cultivates himself in order to bring peace to all people. Cultivating oneself and thereby bringing peace to all people is something even a Yao or a Shun would find difficult."[42]

Kongzi argues this aspect many times in *The Analects* as he exemplifies the right way to govern people. If a ruler follows ritual propriety (*li*), common people will be easily managed by *li*.[43] When Ji Kangzi, a feudal ruler of *Lu*, asked about governing, Kongzi answered, "If you set an example by being correct yourself, who will dare to be incorrect?"[44] Kongzi explained more about the way of governing to Ji Kangzi, commenting that the people do not steal if a ruler does not desire excessively,[45] and that a ruler does not need to use execution if he or she desires goodness.[46] When Zigong asked about governing, Kongzi emphasized three basics: sufficient food, sufficient armaments, and the confidence of the common people. Zigong asked which one is the most important among these, and then, Kongzi valued most confidence because "a state cannot stand once it has lost the confidence of the people."[47] In addition, when Duke Jing of *Qi* asked about governing, Kongzi responded, "Let the lord be a true lord, the ministers true ministers, the fathers true fathers, and the sons true sons."[48] These examples illustrate what Kongzi values in his moral actions, and how he practices Virtues as he recognizes himself as a transmitter. Effortless action in Kongzi is not a coercive way that a person should behave, nor an artificial gesture that someone has to show, but it is the moral action of integrity, sincerity, and

---

42. Ibid., 171, book 14:42.
43. Ibid., book 14:41.
44. Ibid., 133, book 12:17.
45. Ibid, book 12:18.
46. Ibid., 134, book 12:19.
47. Ibid., 128, book 12:7.
48. Ibid., 130, book 12:11.

harmony within human relation. That is Kongzi's ideal, that *junzi* feels at home in *ren* in order to bring peace *to and for* others.

Ren and the Community

Community is another main theme in Confucian ethics, in particular, in the Confucian social thoughts. David B. Wong makes a distinction between community-centered morality and right-centered morality in order to comprehend the sense of community in Confucianism. He defines right-centered moralities as the "recognition of the moral worth of individuals independently of their roles in community," and community-centered moralities as the recognition of "'communal ground' for rights."[49] Although there is a communal ground for rights, both concepts have been debated ceaselessly. The individual democratic rights, such as the right to free speech, to equal education, and to participation in politics, seem to be diminished by community-centered morality. Moreover, the ambiguity of the concept of the common good seems not to fit in this contemporary democratic society. The right-centered theorists, thus, resist the ideal of the ambiguity of a common good in the community-centered ideas. Wong, however, also criticizes these theorists because they simplify the community-centered morality as a form of communitarianism, but they don't fully analyze the complexity of a community.[50] Beyond these criticisms, Wong writes:

> Both right-centered and community-centered traditions need a conception of community that is not based on an unattainable ideal of a shared vision of the common good. This new conception must accept significant diversity and disagreement and must maintain community in spite of that disagreement—not only through the recognition of rights but also through acceptance of the value of accommodation. To accept this value is to seek to find creative ways for conflicting sides within a community to stay within a community and yet not yield entirely to the other. If democratic virtues are needed here, it is not so much the ability to insist on one's right, but the creative ability to negotiate, to give

---

49. Wong, "Rights and Community in Confucianism," in Shun and Wong, *Confucian Ethics*, 32–33.

50. Ibid., 35–43.

and to take, to create solutions that fully satisfy neither side in a conflict but that allow both sides to "save face."[51]

Wong wants to overcome institutionalized forms of both traditions because the institutionalization causes the uniformity of human nature and identity. Then, he values the Confucian virtue of *ren* and its tenet of harmony *within* the common goods, which is shared by a community like moral belief, history, education, arts, politics and economics. With this sense, harmony and *ren* reevaluate conflicts and disagreements in a community which comes from the different conception of the common good, and try to reconcile these gaps within this community.[52] This way of harmony, however, does not institutionalize any ideas of communitarianism nor the individualized rights. Thus, the comprehension of *ren* and community shows the core of the Confucian social ethical thought.

In addition, Joel Kupperman demonstrates that the Confucian concept of community is based on Kongzi's consideration of tradition as his focal motivation of moral action. The principle of tradition is not a simple institutionalized form of rules or ideology, but it is human goodness (*ren*) that comes from human relation. The lifelong process to follow the Way of the Virtue of the Sage Kings is the key to comprehension of the tradition. In this sense of tradition, the value of community has developed through learning as young children follow their parents and their elders, and the parents become their role models. Kupperman explains that

> implicit in the Confucian model is that tradition and community values enter the lives of young children primarily through their parents. Community values do not by themselves constitute goodness; think of the "honest villager." But Confucius would certainly have regarded these rudiments of everyday virtue as a major approach to goodness. An unwillingness to engage in deceit, dishonesty, and violent behavior is, to say the least, required for goodness.... Community values provide categories that structure one's experience of human action.[53]

Tradition is a source of moral modeling as well as moral inspiration for the development of goodness for the self. Ritual and music are the best tools to achieve this moral goodness, and the basis for this practice of music and

51. Ibid., 45.
52. Ibid., 44–46.
53. Kupperman, "Tradition and Community: Formation of the Self," in Shun and Wong, *Confucian Ethics*, 108.

ritual is family, with parents who are the role models for their children in terms of harmonious and virtuous life. With the same account of tradition, community also has a crucial role to play in the moral development of children because not only family, *per se*, is the epitome of community, but also familial relations broaden the social relationship of people in order to practice the Virtue and to obtain moral goodness (*ren*).[54]

Kongzi explains his concept of community based on his appreciation of tradition, as a transmitter of it, and he endeavors to build an ideal society, having its own foundation in the Way of *ren*. To begin with, as I discussed above, Kongzi explains the foundation of *ren* is filial piety (*xiao*) and respect for elderly brothers (*ti*); the initiative of *ren* starts from the familial relationship as people practice rituals (*li*). Filial piety and respect is also the foundation of society, since this familial relationship does not make any limitation within this small group of community, but it is broadened to a further sense of community, i.e., local community, tribes, nations, and empires.[55] This extension occurs when people practice a harmonized life through *li* as the Sage Kings harmonized themselves with *li*. However, because simple harmony sometimes fails in its own value, harmonization has to be founded on *li*.[56] Ritual propriety (*li*) is the source of filial piety (*xiao*) as Kongzi teaches his disciples to obey their parents according to ritual propriety whether their parents are alive or have passed away.[57]

With a similar implication, Kongzi teaches that the governing principle is "to guide a state of one thousand chariots, be respectful in your handing of affairs and display trustworthiness; be frugal in your expenditures and cherish others; and employ the common people only at the proper times."[58] What Kongzi teaches is not to discard or to disrespect any laws or regulations; instead, he places more value on the power of Virtue more as he claims, "When it comes to hearing civil litigation, I am as good as anyone else. What is necessary, though, is to bring it about that there is no civil litigation at all";[59] he also says, "'If excellent people managed the

---

54. Ibid., 114–15.

55. *Analects*, 1, book 1:2.

56. Ibid., 5, book 1:12. Compare this idea with book 13:23. We can read both passages with a similar implication in terms of the comprehension of harmony. Unless harmony is based on *li*, it becomes a simply agreement to others, as the petty person does.

57. Ibid., 9, book 2:5.

58. Ibid., 2, book 1:5.

59. Ibid., 132, book 12:13.

Ren and Ethics

state for a hundred years, then certainly they could overcome cruelty and do away with executions'—how true this saying is!"[60] This governing power does not come from any coercive way, but from the moral instruction of the Way of Virtue.[61] Moreover, this ideal social order is not only the matter of people, but it is also, more significantly, the theme of rulers. For instance:

> Duke Ding asked, "A single saying that can cause a state to flourish—is there such a thing as this?"
> Confucius replied, "There is not saying that can have *that* sort of effect. There is, however, something close. People have a saying, 'Being a ruler is difficult, and being a minister is not easy.' If this saying helps you to understand that being a ruler is difficult, does it not come close to being a single saying that can cause a state to flourish?"[62]

Kongzi stresses again, "If you simply correct yourself, what difficulties could you encounter in government service? If you cannot correct yourself, how can you expect to correct other?"[63] And, Kongzi claims that people broaden the Way,[64] as they take rightness, practice rituals, express modestly, and complete the Way with trustworthy.[65] Kongzi, thus, develops his idea of community as he values *ren* since it formulates an ideal fiduciary community.

All in all, *Ren* is not only the ground of Confucian morality, but also the source to build a fiduciary community and society. For instance, Kongzi develops his idea of *ren* as the basis of his political thought, that is, *ren*-politics. With this sense of *ren*-politics, Kongzi wants to build an ideal society. Thus, morality and ethics is the lifelong process to follow *ren* and the Way of Virtue in order to be a truthful person (*ren*)[66] as well as to formulate an ideal community. Effortless action (*wu-wei*) demonstrates how Confucian moral action obeys *ren*. Through this comprehension of moral action, Kongzi becomes the model of goodness for his next generations, and his

---

60. Ibid., 144, book 13:10.
61. Ibid., 143, book 13:9.
62. Ibid., 145, book 13:15.
63. Ibid., 144, book 13:13.
64. Ibid., 185, book 15:29.
65. Ibid., 181, book 15:18.
66. As I discussed earlier, two Chinese words, person and Goodness, have the same pronunciation, *ren*. I think this is a great coincidence in terms of the study of Confucian ethics because being a human (*ren*) is the process to follow Goodness (*ren*).

action shows us what a community should be, as it is the establishment of humanity. Confucian ethics, thus, explains human relatedness (*ren*) as very significant not only for our individual morality, but also for our conception of community. Based on this study of Kongzi, in the next part, I will explore how Kongzi can have a creative conversation with Levinas in terms of the conception of otherness, the ethical implication of virtue, and the sense of community. Also, I will examine my main argument of the ethics of otherness through this comparative study.

Part IV

The Ethics of Otherness in Levinas and Kongzi

Here, I will examine Levinas's radical alterity and Kongzi's harmonious human relation in order to develop my main argument of the *ethics of otherness*. There are two foci in my argument: human relation in the dialectic of selfhood and otherness; and the narrative characteristic in this human relation in terms of the ethical implication of virtue. I will develop my argument of the ethics of otherness with my comparative study of Levinas and Kongzi based on these two foci—the dialectic of selfhood and otherness and its narrative characteristic in human relation.

I will compare what is the commonality in their understanding of human relation, and what are the differences in their comprehensions of narrative. Through this comparative study, I will argue that the ethics of otherness is not simply based on mutual reciprocity in human relation; rather it is based on the moral conception of the narrative characteristic of selfhood, otherness, and community, through the discernment of humanity as moral humanity.

First, I will deploy my main argument of the *ethics of otherness* as I compare the ethical features in Levinas and Kongzi in terms of their dialectic of selfhood and otherness and its narrative characteristic. As I discussed above, Levinas and Kongzi develop their ethical thoughts based on otherness and human relatedness. Their analyses of the face of the Other and human relatedness (*ren*) will engage my argument of the ethics of otherness. In a sense, Kongzi will have conversation with Levinas as a counterpart of the Euro-American understanding of the ethics in otherness. In another

Part IV: The Ethics of Otherness in Levinas and Kongzi

sense, Kongzi will interpret Levinas with his own conceptualization of *ren*, as another core of otherness.

Lastly, I will explore how Levinas and Kongzi communicate with each other in terms of *response-ability* and the Virtue of *ren*. I will demonstrate that the conversation of Levinas and Kongzi shows a concrete foundation of the ethics of otherness based on their thought of moral humanity, selfhood narrative, community narrative, and the ethical implication of virtue. Thus, I will demonstrate that the ethics of otherness is not simply initiated by the conception of reciprocity, but it is more an accounting on radical otherness and human relatedness, as I delve into the conception of otherness and morality in Kongzi and Levinas.

Chapter 8

Kongzi vs. Levinas

THE CONVERSATION OF RICOEUR and Levinas shows us the fundamental philosophical question of the Euro-American tradition—that is, "What is going on between the self and the other as the beings in the world?" This question tells us a clear distinction between Levinas and Kongzi about how they distinctively or similarly interpret humanity and otherness. Here, I will reevaluate Kongzi's basic question of his philosophy, "What kind of person do I have to be in and for the world?" I will explore the commonality and difference between Levinas and Kongzi based on these two different questions. In this chapter, I will examine their concept of selfhood, human relation, and ethical features as I compare Levinas with Kongzi.

Selfhood, Relation, and Justice

Kongzi's question of "what kind of *person* do *I* have to be in and for the world?" can be modified with Levinasian terms as such: "what kind of *personhood* does *the I* have to have in and for the world?" This modification demonstrates a clear distinction between Kongzi and Levinas. The Euro-American philosophical tradition focuses on the universal norms and the phenomenon of human existence. In particular, the twentieth-century philosophical question concentrates on the issue of human existence, that is, ontology. Here is a similar philosophical attitude in Levinas with this modified philosophical question, "What kind of *personhood* does *the I* have to have in and for the world?" which is based on the inquiry of ontology. First, what does the word "person" imply? Second, who is *the I* as the center of this personhood? Third, how does *the I* identify himself or herself?

Part IV: The Ethics of Otherness in Levinas and Kongzi

Based on these questions, Levinas develops his philosophical analysis as he focuses on selfhood and otherness. When *the I* encounters the other, he or she is able to respond to the Other. *The I* becomes true "I/self" through this encounter of the Other, in particular, the face of the Other. The conceptualization of *the I*, thus, manifests selfhood and otherness. In this sense, Levinas can turn the question back to Kongzi, changing "What kind of person do I have to be *in and for* the world?" into "What is your sense of identity in order to become a good person?" and "What is your comprehension of human relatedness between the self and the other?" The issues of identity, selfhood, and intersubjectivity are proposed in these questions.

Although Levinas disagrees with the priority of identity of Sameness in his critique of totality and ontology in his analysis of Western egology,[1] the issue of identity is a prerequisite in the study of individuality, equality, justice, and ethics. The Levinasian notion of *the I*, as the subject in response to the face of the Other, demonstrates the manifestation of individuality as the underpinning of humanity and morality. On the contrary, in the Confucian tradition, the comprehension of identity is not explicitly mentioned by Kongzi, since ancient China was not a individual-based society, but a relation-based society.[2] This implication of relation-based social values, however, does not mean that Kongzi ignores individuality in the issue of identity. Paradoxically, relation-bounded social value is the basis of individuality and identity in Kongzi, in that Kongzi's initiative of cultivating-self is originated by the conceptualization of *ren*, that is, human relatedness.

Most of all, the different understanding of humanity between Levinas and Kongzi is initiated by their distinctive philosophical foundations: the face of the Other and *ren*. Levinas counts on the phenomenality and trace of the face of the Other in order to interpret selfhood and otherness. The face makes the I respond to the summon of the face, that is, of the Infinity. This is the calling of alterity, which leads the I to become a true self in the world. Thus, human relation is not reciprocal, but asymmetrical, in that selfhood (ipseity) is manifested by the ethical responsibility to otherness (alterity). Inter-subjectivity occurs in this dialectic of selfhood and otherness. On the contrary, Kongzi initiates his philosophical examination from human relatedness (*ren*), and he develops his thought of selfhood and otherness based on this conception of *ren*. In a sense, Kongzi has a profound distinction between

---

1. Levinas, *Totality and Infinity*, 33–52

2. King, "The Individual and Group in Confucianism," in Munro, *Individualism and Holism*, 63.

selfhood and otherness because *ren* makes the self account on the other. In another sense, Kongzi does not have any differentiation between the self and the other, in that his philosophical initiation on human relatedness (*ren*) does not distinguish the self from the other, and vice versa. So, Kongzi develops his philosophical thoughts as he examines human community and politics, that is, *ren*-politics, rather than concentrating on selfhood and otherness. Also, this philosophical concentration on community and politics makes Kongzi ask the question, "What kind of person do I have to be *in and for* the world?" Hence, the face of the Other and *ren* cause Levinas and Kongzi to have different approaches to humanity, human relation, and morality.

The issue of identity and individuality comes from the comprehension of body or flesh as the container of mind and/or spirit. In the Confucian tradition, there is no dualistic approach to body and soul, compared to the Euro-American tradition. The human body is, in a sense, a part of nature. In another sense, the body is the center of the world, as it implicitly contains the concept of spirit or soul, as it beholds *tien-ming* (the Heavenly Mandate) or *qi* (vital essence).[3] The idea of *qi* is one of key concepts to understand human body in the Confucian tradition. Kongzi, however, did not fully articulate the idea of *qi* in the *Analects*. He mentioned *qi* in book 16:7 in the *Analects*, as it implies a kind of motivation of force. Instead, Mengzi developed this idea of *qi* more profoundly in *Mengzi* 2A2, which is translated as *material force* or *vital essence*. Qi is usually understood as an emotional force that makes people become courageous, but sometimes it makes people fall into a fury such as when it is used for revenge. Mengzi explains that *qi* is a fluid which is found in the atmosphere and the human body, and connected with kindness or intensity of one's emotions. Mengzi emphasizes that cultivation of *qi* is critical since it is the basis of the doctrine of human will. Then, he says, "I am good at cultivating my floodlike *qi*." He articulates about his floodlike *qi*, as saying that

> it is a *qi* that is supremely great and supremely unyielding. If one cultivates it with uprightness and does not harm it, it will fill up the space between Heaven and Earth. It is a *qi* that harmonizes with righteousness and the way. Without these, it starves. It is produced by accumulated righteousness. It cannot be obtained by a seizure of righteousness. If some of one's actions leave one's heart unsatisfied, it will starve.[4]

3. Munro, *Concept of Man in Early China*, ch. 3. "The Confucian Concept of Man."
4. *Mengzi*, 39, book 2A2.

He explains the way to cultivate the flood-like *qi* as it should be cultivated as naturally as it can. If someone does something excessively, it will be ruined and even become malice. Because humans and Heaven are united, people can cultivate his or her *qi* toward the world through the way of righteousness; that is, action with humanity (*ren*) is the best way to cultivate it.

In addition, Kongzi explains the concept of human body with the Chinese words *ji* and *shen* while he teaches the Way of *ren* in *The Analects*. Chinese characters *ji* and *shen* illustrate the concept of the human body; however, it does not simply imply the human body or flesh as in the Euro-American tradition, instead, it implies human subjectivity as the basis of self-cultivation. For instance, in *The Analects* book 1:4, Kongzi mentions that he examines himself (*shen*) three times in a day in order to cultivate himself. Book 6:28 says that to establish and to enlarge oneself (*ji*) is to establish and to enlarge others. *Kejifuji* (restraining yourself and returning to the rites constitutes Goodness) in book 12:1 and *shujianren* (cultivating himself [*ji*] and bringing peace to all people) in book 14:42 are significant examples for Kongzi's conceptualization of individuality, identity, and subjectivity. The words of body in Chinese, *shen* and *ji*, thus, do not only mean human body, but they also imply human subjectivity.

The issue of equality and justice leads to questioning Kongzi's comprehension of social hierarchy in terms of the issue of social ontology. The concepts of the self, the Other, and the third party (*illeity*) in Levinas are the sources of social justice. The notion as a transmitter of the tradition of the Sage Kings in ancient China in Kongzi seems not to assure justice between people in their social relationships, in that Kongzi seems to support the social hierarchy in his notion of tradition as valuing the imperial power. In a sense, Kongzi's thought of human relation is based on the social acceptance of human status such as emperor-servant, father-son, husband-wife, older and younger brother, and friends.[5] For Kongzi, the interpretation of human relation, however, is not ontological, but functional, because *ren* is the foundation of these relationships rather than social ontology. Here, Kongzi answers this issue of justice and social hierarchy with the explanation of *junzi* and his political ideals of *ren*-politics within his thought of *ren*.

First, the concept of *junzi* demonstrates the *ren*-bounded human relation. Kongzi exemplifies *junzi* who contains moral goodness (*ren*) and follows the Way of *ren* (humanness). To be a *junzi* is not only the *telos* of

---

5. In *Analects*, these relations are mentioned implicitly, but later, Mengzi generalizes these five relationships in *Mengzi*, 71, book 3A4.8.

Kongzi, but also the lifelong process to practice the Virtue and the Way of *ren*. *Junzi* has the practical sense of human relation as he or she cultivates him or herself according to the Way. In a sense, the concept of *junzi* reveals that Kongzi's social ideals are based on an elite-oriented foundation because *junzi* is a kind of epitome who has moral excellence and rules or teaches commoners with their senses of moral excellence. What *junzi* wants to be, however, is not to obtain any social power, nor to formulate social hierarchy, but it is to comprehend *ren*, and to practice it in order to follow *tien-ming* in their social relations. The more important truth in Kongzi's teaching about *junzi* is that to be a *junzi* is very difficult, but if someone practices *ren* constantly, anybody can become *junzi*, the exemplary person. This teaching demonstrates that Kongzi does not have any ontological sense of social hierarchy. For instance, Kongzi did not make any limitation for any social class in his school. He received many common or lower-class people as his disciples. His most beloved disciple, Yan Hui, was from the lower class. Zhonggong was also a lower-class people. Zilu was a warrior in a local area of *Lu*. The ideal of *junzi*, thus, does not intend to formulate any hierarchical social orders, but it is the manifestation of the question of "what kind of person do I have to be *in and for* the world?"

Ren-politics in Kongzi also does not ensure the permanent socio-ontological status in human relation, in particular, in the relation between the emperor and the servant. Politics are a very complex agenda between Levinas and Kongzi, in that both philosophers have a completely different approach on discourse.[6] The Levinasian conception of discourse between people is a prerequisite to justice, and to grasping the crux of ethics. With the Euro-American sense of politics, Kongzi's *ren*-politics does not fit into this contemporary democratic society related to the issue of human rights like individual freedom, equality and justice.[7] In order to reevaluate Kongzi's political thought, however, it is necessary for us to read the cultural and historical conception of ancient China and Kongzi's approach to this social

6. Levinas does not develop his philosophical thought thoroughly into the realm of politics, not because of his ignorance of politics, but because of his concerns of the philosophical interpretation of ethics in terms of the issue of justice. Instead, Arendtian thought of politics, politics of plurality, has a similar implication with Levinas, in that Arendt values political action as speech and/or discourse in her book *The Human Condition*. Arendt points out the limitation of politics of identity in the Western tradition as she noting the difference between the social and the political. Then, she develops her political thoughts based on the human action of speech and/or discourse.

7. Twiss, "A Constructive Framework for Discussing Confucianism and Human Right," in De Bary and Tu, *Confucianism and Human Rights*, 27–33.

background.⁸ Kongzi lived through one of most chaotic periods in the history of ancient China, that is, he experienced many wars, so survival was the main concern of people. During this period, Kongzi's political thought was very unique and radical, in that Kongzi valued humanity rather than power, then, tried to build an ideal society for people. With this sense, there are two foci in his *ren*-politics: *li* (ritual propriety) and *shu* (understanding of others). Politics in Kongzi is not a personal or a group achievement to obtain political power, but it is the practice of *ren* for people with *li* and *shu*. Kongzi mentions several times the biggest virtue of a ruler is *li* and *shu* in *The Analects* as the rulers follow the great examples of the Sage Kings in ancient China. Kongzi argues the virtuous ruler makes people happy, and then, the kingdom flourishes. On the contrary, the loss of a kingdom is also in the hand of the ruler. Within this sense, Kongzi does not support the permanent hierarchical social order; instead, he implicitly supports regime changes unless the ruler governs people with *ren*.⁹ This implies that the basis of Kongzi's *ren*-politics is people rather than a particular ruler. *Ren*-politics in Kongzi, thus, values humanity, that is, the manifestation of justice. Thus, equality and democratic politics are the sources of justice in the Euro-American tradition; whereas, *ren*-politics, founded on *li* and *shu*, is the foundation on the Confucian concept of justice.

Otherness, Moral Action, and Ethics

The interpretation of human relation is a common ground between Levinas and Kongzi. Neither accounts on mutual reciprocity more than on otherness. Both philosophers disagree with Ricoeur's valuation of mutual reciprocity as the establishment of human relation. Ricoeur's methodology of dialectic of *idem*-identity/*ipse*-identity and the dialectic of selfhood/otherness are based on the phenomenological ontology which credits self-attestation with both self-esteem and self-respect in terms of the ethical conception of otherness. For Levinas, however, humanity, in particular moral humanity, can be jeopardized by this ontological priority on subjectivity to others, related to totalitarianism. Otherness, thus, becomes a

---

8. Ibid., 34–35.

9. See *Analects*, 138–52, book 13 (esp. phrases 2, 3, 4, 6, 8, 9, 11, 12, 13, 15, 17) in order to read Kongzi's political thoughts. More interestingly, Mengzi developed *ren*-politics more radically, as he supports the regime change of a kingdom if a ruler does not follow this *ren*-politics for governing people with *ren* in *Mengzi*, 187, book 7B14.

more radical agenda in his philosophical anthropology rather than reciprocity. Radical otherness assures human relation, in that it obliges the I to respond to the face of the Other, the Infinity, that is, the source of human relation, intersubjectivity. Likewise, Kongzi does not account for mutual reciprocity in his thought of *ren* (human relatedness). Instead, Kongzi puts the initiative of human relatedness on his philosophical anthropology with harmonious co-relation between people as well as between humanity and nature. The etymology of *ren*, per se, demonstrates that human being exists innately as relational being, which means the self cannot stand without the other. The first passage of the *Analects* about three joyful moments in *junzi*, that is, the theme of Kongzi's teaching, also speaks of the existence of my friends is the joyful moment when these friends visit him from far away.[10] Also, Kongzi's account on otherness is shown in his teaching of *li* (ritual propriety), *shu* (understanding of others), and *ren*-politics. The priority of otherness, thus, is the common ground of Levinas and Kongzi.

Their accounts on otherness, however, do not have the same implication in their acceptance of the other. Kongzi's consistent endeavor of equilibrium (*zhong-yong*) is another key in order to understand his interpretation of human relation. Again, the third joyful moment of *junzi* speaks of this harmonious endeavor in human relation for Kongzi, as he says, "To be patient even when others do not understand—is this not the mark of the gentleman (*junzi*)?" Although Kongzi values otherness as the basis of human relation, he tries not to overemphasize otherness as he maintains his kernel question, "What kind of person do I have to be *in and for* the world?" Kongzi's steadfastness of human relationship, thus, reveals this thought of equilibrium as such: "I am living *for* others in the world. But, if I lose myself, I cannot hold *ren* while I am living *in* the world."[11] Kongzi values otherness and human relation based on his lifelong philosophical and political journey for *ren* with the sense of equilibrium.

On the contrary, Levinas's otherness is even more radical than Kongzi. The face of the Other reveals otherness as the Infinity. The epiphany of the face summons me to respond to others. This is the new beginning of ethics as "first philosophy" rather than ontology. Kongzi comments about Levinas's thought of radical otherness with a different sense of Ricoeur's critique of Levinas. Here is a very famous passage in the *Analects*. When his disciple Zigong compared Zizhang with Zixia, Kongzi mentioned that "Zizhang

---

10. *Analects*, 1, book 1:1
11. This sentence is mine from my interpretation of Kongzi.

overshoots the mark, while Zixia falls short of it." Upon hearing this comment, Zigong valued Zizhang more than Zixia. Yet, Kongzi answered that "overshooting the mark is just as bad as falling short of it."[12]

Within this sense, Levinas overshoots the mark with two critical points from Kongzi: Levinas's conceptualization of an-archy, hostage, substitution, and heteronomy misses an equilibrium in human relation; and the exteriority of the Other does not encourage the I as he or she ruminates themselves with their own ethical narratives. Kongzi speaks to Levinas in this way: "From the beginning, there is human relation. I cannot stand here without others, but I am not a hostage of the other. In the equilibrium, I don't have to think of the difference of autonomy and heteronomy. In a sense, I am autonomous because of my relation with others. In another sense, I am heteronomous because of my relation with others." As Ricoeur criticizes Levinas, Kongzi's idea of overshooting illustrates that Levinasian ethics is in the normative category or in the universal principles, although Levinas does not value responsibility within this categorization at all. Also, Levinas's overshooting does not clarify whether or not Levinasian self develops his or her own narratives *in and for* their communities as the foundation of moral actions and ethics.

Responsibility and effortless action (*wu-wei*) / timely action show another different understanding of otherness and morality between Levinas and Kongzi. Effortless action and timeliness in Kongzi are the foundation of moral action in order to fulfill human heartedness (*ren*), based on ritual propriety (*li*), understanding others (*shu*), and harmonious equilibrium (*zhong-yong*). The Euro-American tradition criticizes this ethical conception of moral action in the Confucian tradition as a relativistic or situational approach to human morality without the universal principle or normativity. From the Greek philosophical tradition to the modern Euro-American world, there are certain "all-embracing" principles like mathematical propositions, such as Goodness in Plato, happiness in Aristotle, categorical imperative (duty) in Kant, utilitarian happiness (goal) in Mill, absoluteness of human spirit in Hegel, equality and justice in Marx, and the divine commandment in Judaism and Christianity.[13] The existential philosophers in the late modern period, like Kierkegaard, Nietzsche, and Heidegger, began to criticize this epistemological understanding of human morality which is based on the universal principles. They argued that the authenticity of human beings, which

---

12. *Analects*, book 11:16, 117.
13. Munro, *Concept of Man in Early China*, 57.

concentrates on human subjectivity, is prior to the universal principles. These philosophers replaced the prime position of the universal principles to the supreme authenticity of human existence. The postmodern philosophers start their works with doubting this absolute account on the authenticity of the human being. Among these groups, Levinas is salient in that his thought of radical alterity opens this postmodern understanding of humanity. Based on this phenomenality of the face of the Other, Levinas demonstrates that responsibility is the main key to fulfill humanity.

In a sense, timeliness and effortlessness can be found in Levinas's notion of the phenomenon of the other's face, in that my *response-ability* is the matter of timeliness and effortlessness, as such that the summon of the Other precedes my individual effort. This conceptualization of responsibility in Levinas, however, cannot fully be matched to the Confucian concept of timeliness and effortlessness, since Levinas's argument cannot be separated from the Euro-American epistemological or phenomenological interpretation of human morality. Levinas's responsibility shows us the absoluteness of ethics, in that the claim that the self becomes a hostage of the Other has an implication of total altruism, although he rejects all-embracing universality in Western ontology. Although the total responsibility for the Other builds a new human relation of asymmetry, still this relation is based on the concept of subject to subject relation, that is, it primarily values the response of ipseity (selfhood) toward alterity (otherness). On the contrary, timeliness and effortlessness in Kongzi do not absolutize any part in human relation of both the subject and the other. Kongzi tries not to make any dichotomy in human relation. In this sense, the foundation of human relation in Kongzi is not similar to the conception of intersubjectivity, in particular, to the conceptualization of selfhood and otherness in Levinas. Instead, Kongzi's idea of intersubjectivity is the harmonious life that the individuals need to cultivate themselves through the process of human heartedness (*ren*), and the society and community are flourished by the harmonious lives in this human relation. There is no clear distinction between the individual, the other, and the community in Kongzi. This harmonious life sometimes emphasizes selfish reactions, but other times it emphasizes altruism. Sometimes it tells us of enthusiastic participation in politics, but other times departing from it. In every time, however, Kongzi emphasizes understanding of others (*shu*) and ritual propriety (*li*) in human relationship. The dissimilarity in the understanding of human relation between Kongzi and Levinas, thus, is so distinctive such that Kongzi does not absolutize any part of humanity in the moral action, but Levinas formulates another kind of universal principle in terms of the ethics of responsibility.

The issue of moral character is another focal matter of the conception of the self as the moral agency, *acting by himself or by herself*. The self as moral character is a fundamental thought in both Levinas and Kongzi. Both philosophers, however, do not value the self as the *host or initiative* on moral action in terms of the agenda of moral character, in that moral character, as aiming at a good life, is basically *relational*. Namely, the moral self cannot draw his or her moral character into their everyday life without the relation *with and for* the other. In this sense, the issue of moral character for both philosophers is related to the ideas of social morality rather than normativity. Although Levinas demonstrates that moral character is founded on social morality rather than normativity, his ethics of responsibility does not fully evaluate the social morality in comparison with Kongzi. MacIntyre's question of the tradition of Western emotivism appears in this issue of social morality.[14] "What does 'social' mean?"[15] Sociality is not in the level of self-consciousness nor self-responsiveness for others, but it is based on my everyday practice.[16] Levinas misses the communal narratives between the self and the other in his ethics of responsibility, that the self gets his or her moral character, that is, "social morality" through these narratives. By the way, Kongzi consistently demonstrates that a person has to value this communal narrative while he or she practices *li* and *shu* in their everyday life, that is, Kongzi's way of self-cultivation, such as restraining-self and returning to ritual propriety, and cultivating-self for comforting others. Although Kongzi does not explicitly discuss justice or equality as the basis of moral action, the sense of justice infiltrates the endeavor to practice *ren*, as he follows the Way of Virtue. The ethical distinction between Levinas and Kongzi, thus, is based on their conception of the ethical practice of moral action. Both philosophers disagree with normativity, but support social morality. The ethics of responsibility, however, does not fully value social morality, in that it misses communal narratives in its moral action of responsibility.

---

14. MacIntyre, *After Virtue*, chs. 2 and 3.

15. This question is mine, based on my reading of MacIntyre.

16. MacIntyre, *After Virtue*, 22. This sentence comes from MacIntyre as his basic argument of his book *After Virtue*, and I rephrase this sentence according to my own intention in order to develop my argument of Kongzi's account on virtue.

Overall, the different presupposed questions, "What is going on between the self and the other as beings in the world?," and "What kind of person do I have to be *in and for* the world?" distinguish the notion of selfhood, otherness, and ethics between Levinas and Kongzi. Levinas's account on the face of the Other formulates ethics of responsibility based on his interpretation of otherness. On the contrary, Kongzi's comprehension of *ren* develops the ethical senses of human relatedness in terms of the issue of identity, justice, and sociality, as valuing the narratives between the self, the other, and community. These questions of Levinas and Kongzi lead us to ask some more detail questions, such as how we scrutinize ethics and humanity, how we value ourselves in this ethical foundation, and how we comprehend others in terms of ethics. Based on these questions, I will examine my own argument of *ethics of otherness* in terms of response-ability and the narratives of virtue in Levinas and Kongzi in the next chapter.

Chapter 9

The Ethics of Otherness

Response-ability and the Narrative of Virtue

I WILL DEMONSTRATE IN this chapter my thesis of the ethics of otherness—that is, an anthropological comprehension of ethics: humanity as moral humanity. I will explore the dialectic of selfhood and otherness through the comparison of Levinas's conception of response-ability and Kongzi's thought of Virtue and *ren*. In particular, I will examine the narrative implication in the dialectic of selfhood and otherness, and the interpretation of Virtue and *ren* through this comparison of Levinas and Kongzi.

Humanity as Moral Humanity

The foundation of ethics is anthropology since ethics is based on our understanding of humanity rather than on the study of human morality. On the one hand, ethics is like an artwork of humanity which harmonizes different sounds, colors, and performances without any stagnant or coercive method. On the other hand, ethics is like traveling to a strange place where we can meet others and understand differences. Truly, ethics is not a simple theory of human morality, but it is a comprehension of humanity. In particular, the *ethics of otherness* is based on our anthropological understanding of the manifestation of humanity as *moral humanity*. Ethics looks into humanity from the philosophical norms as Ricoeur analyzes the traditions of Aristotle and Kant in order to find humanness in ethics with the dialectic of *idem/ipso* identities and the dialectic of selfhood and otherness. Also, ethics asks where humanity goes from the examination of human existence

The Ethics of Otherness

of the late modern philosophers, like Kierkegaard, Nietzsche, Husserl, and Heidegger. These questions of humanity concern the pathway of humanity as philosophers seek the way of ethics *for* humanity. I believe that the ethics of otherness is a way for this journey of ethics, in that it does not only evaluate selfhood and otherness from various cultural traditions, but it also revalues otherness and human relation in order to find a way of ethics. The encounter of Levinas and Kongzi is significant for this study of the ethics of otherness, because both philosophers legitimately comprehend otherness and ethics, and they develop their ethical thoughts based on the conceptualization of humanity as moral humanity.

Levinas asked "is ontology fundamental?" in order to evaluate humanity. This question of human existence led Levinas to think "what is at stake in humanity?" What Levinas observed was the jeopardized humanity and the possibility of total negation of being through his experience of the Holocaust. So, Levinas scrutinizes the meaning of human existence, ontology, then, he articulates his philosophical anthropology in terms of ethics rather than ontology. He argues that the problem of Western ontology is prioritization of the self, as opposed to the other, and this prioritization makes it possible for a person to centralize power coercively and to formulate tyranny for ruling over humanity, that is, totalitarian regime. The fundamental belief of totalitarianism, "everything is possible," dehumanizes humanity and the dictator stirs up the masses to become mobs as they can do any kind of inhumane deed with the pretext of the glory of the totalitarian regime.[1] What Levinas heard is the voice from the face of the Other, "Thou shall not kill." The response to the face of the Other, "Here I am," for Levinas, is ethical rather than ontological, in that responsibility is the ethical recognition of the only thing that the I is able to do. The response-ability of the I assures humanity as moral humanity. The relation of the I to the other and others is asymmetry as the basis of ethics. The face summons the I to respond to others, and leads the I to be a moral-self. The inhumane condition in humanity, caused by the egology in the Western ontology, thus, has to be rectified by this acknowledgment of humanity as moral humanity. The way to be human is the acknowledgment of the ethical responsibility of the I to others. This is the reason why Levinas cites Dostoevsky many times, "*We are all responsible for all men before all, and I more than all the others.*"[2] In this sense, Levinas insists: "To be human

---

1. Arendt, *Origins of Totalitarianism*, ch. 12.
2. This citation on Dostoevsky is from *Ethics and Infinity*, 101.

means to live as if one were not a being among beings.... Responsibility is what is incumbent on me exclusively, and what, *humanly*, I cannot refuse. This charge is a supreme dignity of the unique."[3] Hence, Levinas demonstrates humanity as moral humanity.

As Levinas experienced life-threatening moments, Kongzi experienced the consistent threatening of death, caused by consecutive wars, while he lived the Spring and Fall Period in ancient China. This experience of extreme threat made Kongzi ask himself, "What kind of person do I have to be *in and for* the world?" What Kongzi discerned was the inhumane condition and the struggle of humanity for survival during this war period. This discernment made Kongzi examine the foundation of humanity, and he acknowledged *ren* is the basis of humanity. Kongzi tried to participate in the real political arena in order to actualize his conception of *ren* into the real human situation. He could obtain a position, as a chief counselor of the king, in his home country *Lu*; however, he failed to expend his ideal of *ren*-politics. He was exiled from his country, and wandered through other countries like *Chou*, *Qi* and *Wei*. Politicians and kings respected him as an admirable politician, but he failed to get another political position because his ideal was considered unrealistic. He was frustrated because of this situation; however, he did not give up his thoughts of *ren* and his desire to build an ideal society.[4] Kongzi valued *ren* as his philosophical foundation, in that *ren* ensures the significance of humanity, that is, human relatedness. Fundamentally, humanity is relational. Life is the ongoing way to learn this human relation, and to cultivate self in order to understand others (*shu*) and to participate in rituals (*li*). This is why Kongzi teaches consistently the Way of Virtue as he says, "Virtue is never solitary; it always has neighbors."[5] Kongzi's personal conviction of his life, "at fifteen, I set mind upon learning; ... and at seventy, I could follow my heart's desires without overstepping the bounds of propriety,"[6] is not a simple personal confession of his life; rather, it demonstrates his comprehension of humanity. For Kongzi, thus, life is the way of humanity to make oneself as moral humanity.

3. Levinas, *Ethics and Infinity*, 100–101.

4. Chin, *Authentic Confucius*. After his death, he was able to obtain reevaluation and his thought of *ren*-politics became the main idea in Chinese politics. Unfortunately, the followers of Kongzi and the Chinese politicians could not follow what Kongzi taught about *ren*-politics in the *Analects*. Instead, Confucianism became another ruling ideology to support the social hierarchy. For more, see Fung, *Short History of Chinese Philosophy*.

5. *Analects*, 37–38, book 4:25.

6. Ibid., 9, book 2:4.

Hence, both philosophers conceptualize humanity as moral humanity within the dialectic of selfhood and otherness. The self acknowledges his or her humanity as they recognize otherness as the foundation of their moral action. Humanity becomes genuine human being, not because the self obtains the ego-centric authenticity, but because the self acknowledges otherness and humanness as moral humanity. For Levinas, the response-ability of the I to the summon of the face of the Other leads the self to be a human as a moral-self. For Kongzi, the discernment of the Way of *ren* and the process of self-cultivation lead humanity to be a being as a moral-self. This is the dialectic of selfhood and otherness in both philosophers, in which humanity becomes aware of his or her humanness in this dialectic of selfhood and otherness, regarding humanity as moral humanity. The ethics of otherness, thus, is based on this anthropological interpretation of humanity as moral humanity.

Response-ability and the Narrative of Virtue

My final argument of the *ethics of otherness* is the dialectic in the conceptualizing process of responsibility and *ren*, based on the dialectic of Levinas's and Kongzi's interpretation of humanity as moral humanity. Now, I will examine both Levinas's conception of response-ability and Kongzi's valuation on the narrative of Virtue in *ren*. With the sense of moral humanity, I will explore how Levinas's conception of *response-ability* ensures the idea of selfhood narrative, and how Kongzi's proposal of *ren* manifests the Way of Virtue. Then, I will see what they share in common, and how they listen to each other, in order to develop the idea of the ethics of otherness. This is the fruit of the ethical implication of Virtue in Kongzi, and the moral significance of selfhood narrative in Levinas. This exploration will articulate that the crux of the ethics of otherness is my response-ability and the narrative of Virtue in *ren* within the dialectic of selfhood and otherness.

MacIntyre articulates the feature of narrative selfhood as he explains the issue of moral agency, and he notes that the agent not only writes his or her ethical character as an author, but he or she also acts their ethical character as an actor, who contains both intelligibility/accountability as well as personal identity.[7] MacIntyre emphasizes that "what the agent is able to do and say intelligibly as an actor is deeply affected by the fact that we are never more (and sometimes less) than the coauthors of our

---

7. MacIntyre, *After Virtue*, 212–13, 217–18.

own narratives."[8] Furthermore, "the form of narratives is appropriate for understanding the actions of others," because "we all live out narratives in our lives."[9] Then he points out the twofold requirement of the concept of narrative of selfhood: the subject of a history is *the I* and my action has its own peculiar meaning; and the narrative of selfhood is "correlative," which means that I am not only accountable to the story, but I am also a part of *their* story.[10] The agent, who has personal identity, becomes intelligible and accountable within the narrative between the self and the other. Then MacIntyre goes back to his initial philosophical question of human action and identity as he notes that "the unity of a human life is the unity of a narrative quest."[11] Narrative requests three boundaries, in terms of virtue and moral identity, such as the good life, practices, and membership in communities.[12] MacIntyre demonstrates that I am a part of history as a bearer of a tradition. Then he asks, "What sustains and strengthens traditions," as a living tradition? He answers that the possession virtue is "knowing how to select among the relevant stack of maxims and how to apply them in particular situations," rather than to get "the knowledge of a set of generalizations or maxims which may provide our practical inferences with major premises."[13] This answer does not mean that virtue is always changeable according to various social situations, but it means that virtue is based on selfhood narrative with the relation between the self and the others in community as it formulates living traditions.

To begin with, Levinas's interpretation of response-ability speaks of an ethical feature of selfhood narrative in terms of the issue of moral agency. With the sense of moral identity and selfhood narrative, the question of "who?" and the response of this question, to say "here I am," in terms of the issue of moral agency, reveal the narrative characteristic of ethics.[14] Namely, to ask "who?" and to say "here I am" demonstrate a moral characteristic with the moral implications of description for good, prescription for obligatory, and selfhood narrative.[15] Levinas's conception of *response-ability* has

8. Ibid., 213.
9. Ibid., 212.
10. Ibid., 217–18 (italics mine).
11. Ibid., 218–19.
12. Ibid., 219–21.
13. Ibid., 223.
14. Ricoeur, *Oneself as Another*, 167.
15. Ibid., ch. 6.

the sense of selfhood narrative, since the I is obliged to *respond* to the face of the Other, the Infinity, and my response is based on the communication with others. This setting of narrative ensures the inter-human relationship, such that Levinas develops the notion of human relationship in his interpretation of Saying and response-ability. In order to maintain this inter-human relationship, my response-ability has the purest sense of passivity in terms of substitution. This relationship is what Levinas calls "humanity" and "subjectivity."[16] Here, Levinasian selfhood narrative comes into his insightful citation, "I *am* you, whenever I am I." As I discussed already, this narrative can be modified as "I *respond to* you, whenever I am I," that is, it is my *response-ability* as I am saying "here I am." This is the narrative structure in Levinas between selfhood and otherness.

Kongzi exemplifies Virtue in this ethical notion of *wu-wei*, effortless action. Kongzi teaches how our moral practice in Virtue is related to sincerity and harmony in terms of effortless action and timeliness. For instance, *junzi* does not practice Virtue with outward methods in order to demonstrate his or her moral excellence; instead, he or she consistently follows the Way through their everydayness with effortless action. Kongzi says, "The Virtue of a gentleman is like a wind, and the Virtue of a petty person is like the grass—when the wind moves over the grass, the grass is sure to bend."[17] Another good example is in the *Analects*, as "whenever the Master was singing in a group and heard something that he liked, he inevitably asked to have it sung again, and only then would harmonize with it."[18] According to this tenet of Virtue, Kongzi develops his thought of *ren*-politics with this idea of bringing peace through the process of self-cultivation.[19] This is the way of *junzi* as he or she feels "at home in Goodness (*ren*)," since, "without Goodness, one cannot remain constant in adversity and cannot enjoy enduring happiness."[20] Hence, Virtue is the moral action of integrity, sincerity, and harmony within human relations for Kongzi. Virtue is a unique notion in Confucian morality, in that it not only reveals humanness (*ren*), but it also shows a kind of charismatic power to follow the Way of *ren*, that is, the great tradition of the Sage Kings like Yao and Shun in ancient China. For

---

16. Levinas, *Otherwise than Being*, 46.
17. *Analects*, 134, book 12:19.
18. Ibid., 75, book 7:32.
19. Ibid., 171–72, book 14:42.
20. Ibid., 29–30, book 4:2.

Kongzi, thus, Virtue reveals the ethical embodiment of *ren*, the manifestation of human relatedness in terms of the conception of *ren*.

What Levinas discerns is that the response-ability of the I ensures the idea of selfhood narrative; whereas, what Kongzi demonstrates is that *ren* manifests the Way of Virtue. Let's go back to MacIntyre's interpretation of selfhood narrative as it is correlative as a part of *story* in this human relation based on *tradition* and *history*, and his notion of virtue as the sustainer or strengthener for this story in this particular *tradition* or *history*. This is what Levinas and Kongzi have to listen to each other. Levinas conceives the notion of selfhood narrative in terms of response-ability without the ethical implication of Virtue. Kongzi proposes the manifestation of Virtue, but he misses the sense of selfhood narrative. Levinas does not have the sense of story *in and for* his or her community of the self in his conception of response-ability. Even more seriously, he does not have any idea of story between the I and the Infinite, which contains the image of divinity, which means that Levinas's narrative is simply *my* story without the sense of community narrative. For instance, we cannot read the *stories* between Moses and God in the biblical tradition in Levinas's self-narrative of "here I am." In the biblical tradition, Moses and the Divinity had their stories such as the dynamics of God's summon, Moses' hesitation, God's reassurance, and Moses' decision. Levinas's self-narrative, however, has only my heteronomous obedience. We cannot read that the response of the I, to say "here I am," to the Infinite, the other, develops the deeper *stories* of community through the practice of the self and the sense of good for *us* in Levinas. In this sense, Levinas has to listen to how the response-ability of the I is aware of the ethical implication of Virtue and the stories of community from Kongzi.

On the contrary, Kongzi has a unique idea of virtue, as he demonstrates virtue is the Way of *ren*, which is *in* but *beyond* our moral excellence. That is the reason why Confucian terminology of virtue (*de*) is usually capitalized as "Virtue." Virtue has its own story *in* and *for* community according to its history and tradition. Virtue in Kongzi, ironically, does not have the explicit sense of selfhood narrative. Although we read many stories in and for the community in the *Analects*, Kongzi does not tell us "where the self is, and how the self gets the sense of his or her moral identity" in and through the community stories. Even though Kongzi emphasizes self-cultivation in order to follow the Virtue of *ren*, Kongzi does not clarify how the self develops his or her selfhood narrative in their communities. Namely, the self in Kongzi does not speak his or her own stories as a part of history or tradition *in* and *for* their communities. Therefore, Kongzi has to listen to what Levinas says about the selfhood narrative, to say "here I am." Kongzi's main concern of "what kind of person should I have to be *in* and *for* the world?" has to be reassured by Levinas's manifestation of response-ability, "I *am* you, whenever I am I," and my modification of this phrase, "I *respond to* you, whenever I am I." Hence, Levinas has to listen to the stories of community and the narrative of Virtue from Kongzi in the *Analects*; whereas, Kongzi needs to listen to the selfhood narrative from Levinas.

Therefore, ethics is anthropology, as it comprehends humanity as moral humanity. In particular, the *ethics of otherness* is based on this conception of moral humanity, which assures us that humanity is fundamentally relational between selfhood and otherness. Moral humanity is not only the self-attestation as a moral self *in* and *for* the world, but it also is acknowledgment of the social morality in this human relation. The ethics of otherness is the moral dialectic of selfhood and otherness through selfhood narrative, the ethical implication of Virtue, and the story of community. Levinas and Kongzi contribute significantly for this conception of the ethics of otherness in their thoughts of response-ability and the Virtue of *ren*.

Conclusion

IN THIS BOOK, I presented four main discussions for the study of the ethics of otherness: a theoretical foundation in the Euro-American tradition in terms of the conception of mutual reciprocity; the phenomenological comprehension of the face of the Other in Levinas; the signification of *ren* (human relatedness) in Kongzi; and a comparative study, having a creative dialogue between Levinas and Kongzi. I discussed both philosophers' comprehension of otherness and ethics through this book, as I developed my thought of the ethics of otherness.

In the first part, I examined the theoretical interpretation of ethics and otherness as I explored Ricoeur's account on reciprocity and human relation, as I focused mainly on his work *Oneself as Another*. Ricoeur examined the dialectic of *idem*-identity (sameness) and *ipse*-identity (selfhood), then, he explored the dialectic of selfhood and otherness, as he argued that reciprocity and human relation are the basis of the ethics of otherness. Ricoeur developed his ethical thought, analyzing the Aristotelian concept of "good," and the Kantian notion of "obligatory" of the autonomous self. In Ricoeur, ethics is initiated by self-attestation for "good" and "obligatory" through the dialectic of selfhood and otherness. Based on these analyses, Ricoeur argued Levinas did not fully ensure human relation and reciprocity in the idea of radical otherness. Ricoeur criticized that Levinas's radical otherness is hyperbolic and irrelational, in that it over-expresses the Other and separates the self from others. On the contrary, Richard A. Cohen responded to Ricoeur, as he argued that Levinas developed his ethical thought as he demonstrated "humanity" as "moral humanity," prioritizing otherness to selfhood in order to explore the morality of the self. These interpretations of otherness reveal the theoretical comprehension about the ethics of otherness in the Euro-American tradition.

Conclusion

In the second part, I examined the key conception of Levinas's ethical thought, that is, the face of the Other. Levinas explored the significance of the Other's face in his philosophical interpretation of the infinity and the proximity of the face. In particular, the proximity of the Other's face makes people acknowledge his or her responsibility in their inter-human relations. The response of the self to say "here I am" implies that the I does not have an ethical capability to do something good for others, but it reveals my passivity, that is, substitution, as the hostage situation of the self *for* others. Thus, human relation is asymmetrical rather than reciprocal. There is also the third party in this human relation. Sometimes, the third party implies my neighbors, but at other times, it is more than my neighbors. The self is conscious of justice and peace in human relation among the I, the Other, and the third party. Hence, for Levinas, responsibility is the source of ethics, and "first philosophy" is ethics rather than ontology, since the ethics of responsibility manifests human beingness instead of ontology.

In the third chapter, thus, I explored *ren* (human relatedness) in Kongzi, as I examined Kongzi's understanding of humanness in terms of *ren*, his comprehension of human relation related to his conception of the self and the other, and the ethical implication of *ren*. Kongzi developed his philosophy based on his conception of *ren*, and he also envisioned building an ideal community according to *ren*. Namely, for Kongzi, *ren* is not only the source of morality, but also the foundation of a fiduciary community and society. Kongzi explored ways to do self-cultivation according to *ren* through the Way (*tao*) of Virtue (*de*), as he developed his comprehension of Virtue in order to illustrate human relatedness (*ren*). He demonstrated that ethics and *ren* are based on human relation, as he signified ritual propriety (*li*) and understanding of others (*shu*) as not only the source of moral action in terms of effortless action (*wu-wei*), but also the foundation of community and society. In short, Kongzi developed his ethical thought, based on *ren*, as he examined human relatedness through his practical comprehension of the Way of Virtue for community and society.

Lastly, I examined my argument of *ethics of otherness* that it is not based on the manifestation of mutual reciprocity; rather, it is based on of the prioritization of otherness to the self in the dialectic of selfhood and otherness, through my comparative study of Levinas and Kongzi. *Ethics of otherness* is based on the manifestation of humanity as moral humanity, since humanity is relational in the dialectic of selfhood and otherness. Moral humanity is not only based on the process of self-attestation as a moral self, but it also is based on the awareness and assurance of the social morality in human relation. *Ethics of otherness* relies on the moral narrative of selfhood in the dialectic of selfhood and otherness, and the story of community according to the ethical implication of Virtue. Therefore, Levinas and Kongzi significantly demonstrate this conception of *ethics of otherness* through their creative conversation of response-ability and the Virtue of *ren*.

A Comparative Study for the Study of the Ethics of Otherness

I had two goals in this book: a paradigm shift in philosophical studies from the Euro-American-centered approaches to cross-cultural approaches, and a communication between these two different traditions in terms of the study of ethics. My goals were to find a way not only to illuminate the ethical thought of the East Asian tradition into Euro-American ethical thought, but also to have a creative conversation about ethics between both traditions in this global community. Thus, the purpose of this research was not only to compare Levinas with Kongzi about their ethical perspectives, but also to have a creative conversation about the otherness and humanness of both philosophers. With this purpose, I explored their understandings of subjectivity; their assessment of otherness and human relatedness in terms of the conception of intersubjectivity; and their ethical norms like responsibility in Levinas and human-heartedness or benevolence (*ren*) in Kongzi.

My first goal was initiated by my inquiry of selfhood and human relationship in both the Euro-American and East Asian tradition. Euro-American philosophers have developed their notions of human relationship with a consensus idea that self-attestation is the foundation of mutual reciprocity, as I studied Ricoeur as above. When I read Levinas, however, I found that true human relationship cannot be fully guaranteed in the conception of reciprocity, since the prioritization of the self to the other does not value the other as the self; instead, it materializes and marginalizes humanity. Levinas gave me great insight about human relation and ethics, as he demonstrated that the asymmetrical relation is the basis of humanity and ethics. Levinas's interpretation of human relation, however, could not give me a more thorough comprehension of human relation, since his explanation of otherness focuses on the dialectic of selfhood and otherness. In my criticism of Levinas, he is stuck on self-oriented otherness in his conception of responsibility, saying "here I am," to the other, that is, *my*

Conclusion

responsibility for others, as his foundation of ethics. In this sense, I asked myself, "How can I interpret human relation and ethics differently as an East Asian?" I found that the comprehension of *ren* (human relatedness) in Kongzi could give me an answer to my question, in that otherness is the basis of our ethical acknowledgment of human relatedness. Thus, I was able to reach a paradigm shift in ethical studies from the Euro-American self-centered ethical studies to the cross-cultural approaches in ethical studies.

This first goal of my research, however, is not a simple criticism on Levinas from my East Asian perspective, in that I found that Kongzi also misses something important, and has to listen to Levinas. Here, I built the second goal for my dissertation—a creative conversation for both Levinas and Kongzi. Kongzi valued human relatedness (*ren*) in his ethical thought, as he wanted to build an ideal society. He developed his unique thought of Virtue (*de*) as he concentrated on the significance of the Way (*tao*) and the Heavenly Mandate (*tian-ming*). He emphasized that human relatedness (*ren*) had to be practiced by ritual propriety (*li*) and the understanding of others (*shu*) in his conception of moral action, that is, effortless action (*wu-wei*). Through this ethical practice, humanity can formulate the story of community, based on the ethical narrative of *ren* and Virtue *in* and *for* their community. Through this practice, however, the self cannot fully become the core of the community. Therefore, Kongzi must listen to Levinas's dialectic of selfhood and otherness. This is the second goal of this research.

I formulated my thesis in this book based on these two goals, that is, *the ethics of otherness is not simply initiated by the conception of mutual reciprocity; rather, it comes from the acknowledgment and the recognition of the manifestation of otherness*. Throughout this book, I examined the ethical implication of the face of the Other in Levinas, and the significance of human relatedness (*ren*) in Kongzi. Finally, I recaptured the idea that the *ethics of otherness* is not only based on the conception of humanity as moral humanity, but it is also based on the moral dialectic of selfhood and otherness through the selfhood narrative, the ethical implication of Virtue, and the story of community. Levinas and Kongzi, I believe, tell us a significant ethical implication about the *ethics of otherness* through their thoughts of response-ability and the Virtue of *ren*.

Bibliography

Ames, Roger T., and Henry Rosemont, trans. *The Analects of Confucius*. New York: Ballantine, 1998.
Ames, Roger T., et al., eds. *Self as Person in Asian Theory and Practice*. Albany: State University of New York Press, 1994.
Angle, Stephen C. *Sagehood: The Contemporary Significance of Neo-Confucian Philosophy*. Oxford: Oxford University Press, 2009.
Arendt, Hannah. *The Human Condition*. 2nd ed. Chicago: University of Chicago Press, 1998.
———. *The Origins of Totalitarianism*. New York: Harcourt, Brace, 1973.
Bloechl, Jeffrey, ed. *The Face of the Other and the Trace of God: Essays on the Philosophy of Emmanuel Levinas*. New York: Fordham University Press, 2000.
Brooks, E. Bruce, and Brooks A. Taeko, trans. *The Original Analects: Sayings of Confucius and His Successors*. New York: Columbia University Press, 1998.
Chan, Wing-tsit, trans., ed. "The Evolution of the Confucian Concept of *Jen*." *Philosophy East and West* 4 (1955) 295–319.
———. *A Source Book in Chinese Philosophy*. Princeton: Princeton University Press, 1963.
Chin, Annping. *The Authentic Confucius: A Life of Thought and Politics*. New York: Scribner, 2007.
Cline, Erin M. "The Way, the Right, and the Good." *Journal of Religious Ethics* 37 (2009) 107–29.
Cohen, Richard A., and James L. Marsh, eds. *Ricoeur as Another: The Ethics of Subjectivity*. Albany: State University of New York Press, 2002.
Critchley, Simon, and Robert Bernasconi, eds. *The Cambridge Companion to Levinas*. Cambridge: Cambridge University Press, 2003.
———, eds. *Re-reading Levinas*. Indianapolis: Indiana University Press, 1991.
Davis, Colin. *Levinas: An Introduction*. Notre Dame: University of Notre Dame Press, 1996.
De Bary, Wm. Theodore, ed. *Sources of East Asian Tradition*. Vols. 1–2. New York: Columbia University Press, 2008.
De Bary, Wm. Theodore, and Tu Weiming, eds. *Confucianism and Human Rights*. New York: Columbia University Press, 1998.
Derrida, Jacques. *Adieu to Emmanuel Levinas*. Translated by Pascale-Anne Brault and Michael Naas, Stanford: Stanford University Press, 1999.
———. *Writing and Difference*. Translated by Alan Bass. Chicago: University of Chicago Press, 1978.

BIBLIOGRAPHY

Farley, Edward. *Good and Evil: Interpreting a Human Condition*. Minneapolis: Fortress, 1990.

Fingarette, Herbert. *Confucius: The Secular as Sacred*. Prospect Heights, IL: Waveland, 1972.

Fung, Yu-Lan. *A Short History of Chinese Philosophy*. Edited by Derk Bodde. New York: Free Press, 1976.

Gibbs, Robert. *Why Ethics? Signs of Responsibilities*. Princeton: Princeton University Press, 2000.

Grenz, Stanley. *The Social God and the Relational Self*. Louisville: Westminster John Knox, 2001.

Hall, David, and Roger Ames. *Thinking through Confucius*. Albany: State University of New York Press, 1987.

Ivanhoe, Philip. *Confucian Moral Self Cultivation*. Indianapolis: Hackett, 2000.

———. *Ethics in the Confucian Tradition*. Indianapolis: Hackett, 1990.

Jones, James W. "The Relational Self: Contemporary Psychoanalysis Reconsiders Religion." *Journal of the American Academy of Religion* 59 (1991) 119–35.

Kang, Nam-Soon. "Confucian Familism and Its Social/Religious Embodiment in Christianity: Reconsidering the Family Discourse from a Feminist Perspective." *Asia Journal of Theology* 18 (2004) 168–89.

Katz, Claire E., ed. *Emmanuel Levinas: Critical Assessments of Leading Philosophers*. New York: Routledge, 2005.

Kepnes, Steven. "Ethics after Levinas: Robert Gibbs's Why Ethics? Signs of Responsibilities." *Modern Theology* 19 (2003) 103–15.

Lau, D. C., trans. *Confucius: The Analects*. Hong Kong: Chinese University Press, 1983.

Legge, James, trans. *The Chinese Classics*. Vol. 1. Hong Kong: Hong Kong University Press, 1960.

Levinas, Emmanuel. *Alterity & Transcendence*. Translated by Michael B. Smith. New York: Columbia University Press, 1999.

———. *Basic Philosophical Writings*. Edited by Adriaan Peperzak et al. Indianapolis: Indiana University Press, 1996.

———. *Collected Philosophical Paper*. Translated by Alphonso Lingis. Pittsburgh: Duquesne University Press, 1988.

———. *Entre Nous: On Thinking-of-the-other*. Translated by Michael B. Smith and Barbara Harshav. New York: Columbia University Press, 1998.

———. *Ethics and Infinity*. Translated by Richard A. Cohen. Pittsburgh: Duquesne University Press, 1985.

———. *Existence & Existents*. Translated by Alphonso Lingis. Foreword by Robert Bernasconi. Pittsburgh: Duquesne University Press, 2001.

———. *Face to Face with Levinas*. Edited by Richard A. Cohen. Albany: State University of New York Press, 1986.

———. *God, Death, and Time*. Translated by Bettina Bergo. Stanford: Stanford University Press, 2000.

———. *Humanism of the Other*. Translated by Nidra Poller. Introduction by Richard A. Cohen. Chicago: University of Illinois Press, 2006.

———. *In the Time of the Nations*. Translated by Michael B. Smith. New York: Continuum, 1994.

———. *Is It Righteous to Be: Interviews with Emmanuel Levinas*. Edited by Jill Robbins. Stanford: Stanford University Press, 2001.

BIBLIOGRAPHY

———. *The Levinas Reader*. Edited by Sean Hand. Oxford: Blackwell, 1989.
———. *Of God Who Comes to Mind*. Translated by Bettina Bergo. Stanford: Stanford University Press, 1986.
———. *On Escape*. Translated by Bettina Bergo. Stanford: Stanford University Press, 2003.
———. *Otherwise than Being*. Translated by Alphonso Lingis. Pittsburgh: Duquesne University Press, 1998.
———. *Outside the Subject*. Translated by Michael B. Smith. Stanford: Stanford University Press, 1994.
———. *Proper Names*. Translated by Michael B. Smith. Stanford: Stanford University Press, 1996.
———. *Time and the Other*. Translated by Richard A. Cohen. Pittsburgh: Duquesne University Press, 1987.
———. *Totality and Infinity*. Translated by Alphonso Lingis. Pittsburgh: Duquesne University Press, 1969.
———. *Unforeseen History*. Translated by Nidra Poller. Chicago: University of Illinois Press, 2004.
Li, Chenyang. *The Sage and the Second Sex: Confucianism, Ethics, and Gender*. Chicago: Open Court, 2000.
Lingis, Alphonso. *Excesses: Eros and Culture*. Albany: State University of New York Press, 1984.
Liu, Zehua, and Ge Quan. "On the 'Human' in Confucianism." *Journal of Ecumenical Studies* 26 (1989) 313–35.
Llewelyn, John. *Emmanuel Levinas: The Genealogy of Ethics*. New York: Routledge, 1995.
Lovin, Robin W. *Christian Ethics: An Essential Guide*. Nashville: Abingdon, 2000.
Manning, Robert John Sheffler. *Interpreting Otherwise than Heidegger: Emmanuel Levinas's Ethics as First Philosophy*. Pittsburgh: Duquesne University Press, 1993.
MacIntyre, Alasdair. *After Virtue*. 3rd ed. Notre Dame: University of Notre Dame Press, 2007.
Morgan, Michael L. *Discovering Levinas*. New York: Cambridge University Press, 2007.
Munro, Donald J. *The Concept of Man in Early China*. Ann Arbor: Center for Chinese Studies, University of Michigan, 2001.
———, ed. *Individualism and Holism: Studies in Confucian and Taoist Values*. Ann Arbor: Center for Chinese Studies, University of Michigan, 1985.
Niebuhr, Reinhold. *An Interpretation of Christian Ethics*. New York: Meridian, 1956.
———. *Moral Man and Immoral Society*. 3rd ed. Louisville: Westminster John Knox, 2001.
Nyitray, Vivian-Lee. "Confusion, Elision, and Erasure: Feminism, Religion, and Chinese Confucian Traditions." *Journal of Feminist Studies in Religion* 26 (2010) 143–60.
Peperzak, Adriaan Theodoor. *Beyond: The Philosophy of Emmanuel Levinas*. Evanston, IL: Northwestern University Press, 1997.
———. *To the Other: An Introduction to the Philosophy of Emmanuel Levinas*. West Lafayette, IN: Purdue University Press, 1993.
Ricoeur, Paul. *Oneself as Another*. Translated by Kathleen Blamey. Chicago: University of Chicago Press, 1992.
Schrag, Calvin O. *The Self after Postmodernity*. New Haven: Yale University Press, 1997.
Shun, Kwong-loi. "Studying Confucian and Comparative Ethics: Methodological Reflections." *Journal of Chinese Philosophy* 36 (2009) 455–78.

Bibliography

Shun, Kwong-loi, and David B. Wong, eds. *Confucian Ethics: A Comparative Study of Self, Autonomy, and Community.* Cambridge: Cambridge University Press, 2004.

Slingerland, Edward G., trans. *Confucius Analects.* Indianapolis: Hackett, 2003.

———. *Effortless Action:* Wu-wei *as Conceptual Metaphor and Spiritual Ideal in Early China.* Oxford: Oxford University Press, 2003.

———. "Virtue Ethics, the *Analects,* and the Problem of Commensurability." *Journal of Religious Ethics* 29 (2001) 97–125.

Stanford Encyclopedia of Philosophy. "Comparative Philosophy: Chinese and Western." Published July 31, 2001. Revised December 8, 2014. http://plato.stanford.edu/entries/comparphil-chiwes. Accessed December 11, 2010.

Taylor, Mark C., *Altarity.* Chicago: University of Chicago Press, 1987.

———. ed. *Deconstruction in Context: Literature and Philosophy.* Chicago: University of Chicago Press, 1986.

Tillich, Paul. *The Courage to Be.* New Haven: Yale University Press, 2000.

———. *Love, Power, and Justice.* Oxford: Oxford University Press, 1954.

———. *Morality and Beyond.* New York: Harper & Row, 1963.

———. *Systematic Theology.* 3 vols. 3rd ed. Chicago: University of Chicago Press, 1963.

———. *Theology of Culture.* Oxford: Oxford University Press, 1959 and 1964.

Tu, Wei-ming. *Centrality and Commonality: An Essay on Confucian Religiousness.* Albany: State University of New York Press, 1989.

———. *Confucian Thought: Selfhood as Creative Transformation.* Albany: State University of New York Press, 1985.

———. *Humanity and Self-Cultivation: Essays in Confucian Thought.* Boston: Cheng & Tsui, 1998.

Tymieniecka, Anna-Teresa, ed. *The Enigma of Good and Evil; The Moral Sentiment in Literature.* Analecta Husserliana: The Yearbook of Phenomenological Research 85. Dordrecht: Springer, 2005.

Van Norden, Bryan, ed. *Confucius and the Analects: New Essays.* Oxford: Oxford University Press, 2002.

———, trans. *Mengzi.* Indianapolis: Hackett, 2008.

Yao, Xinzhong. *Confucianism and Christianity: A Comparative Study of Jen and Agape.* Brington, UK: Sussex Academic, 1996.

———. *An Introduction to Confucianism.* Cambridge: Cambridge University Press, 2000.

www.ingramcontent.com/pod-product-compliance
Lightning Source LLC
Chambersburg PA
CBHW071505150426
43191CB00009B/1423